In Advance of the Landing: Folk Concepts of Outer Space

★

Abbeville Press

Publishers

New York

In Advance of the Landing:

By Douglas Curran

Folk Concepts of Outer Space

Foreword by Tom Wolfe

For Kate, who left the porch light on,
and my brother Donald,
who never got to see this finished.

Library of Congress Cataloging in Publication Data

Curran, Douglas.
  In advance of the landing.

  Bibliography; p.
  Includes index.
  1. Unidentified flying objects (in religion, folklore,
etc.) I. Title.
TL789.C87 1985   001.9'42   85-9019
ISBN 0-89659-523-4 (pbk.)

First edition

Foreword copyright © 1985 by Tom Wolfe.

Printed and bound in Italy.

Permission to reproduce the comic-
strip frames from "Buck Rogers in the
Twenty-fifth Century" (see pages 8,
19, 127, 130) has been granted by
the Dille Family Trust. The video of
the Los Angeles Olympic Games
ceremonies (see page 121), courtesy
and copyright ABC Sports.

Front cover:
Flying saucer by Jene Highstein, 1980.
Park Forest, Illinois.

Editor: Nancy Grubb
Designer: Karen Salsgiver

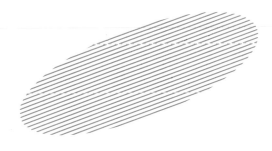

Contents

Foreword

As you are about to see, Douglas Curran is not only a photographer but also a reporter, and an extremely gifted one. I am tempted to suggest that he also qualifies as an anthropologist, but I think I will leave it at "reporter." To be a reporter of Douglas Curran's caliber is a lofty enough achievement. He has discovered an exotic world, and for eight years he has traveled remote terrains throughout the United States and Canada exploring it. This book is the culmination of a quest that, by terrestrial standards, is as extraordinary as that of the people he brings to life in the pages that follow. ★ I ran into such people many times when I was working on *The Right Stuff*, a book about the astronauts, but I never got to know them the way Douglas Curran has. They gravitated to Cape Canaveral, Houston, California, to wherever NASA prepared to probe the heavens. They were not interested in lunar geology, solar energy stations, or the psychology of the astronauts, which happened to be the subject that interested me. They looked upon astronauts not as extraordinary adventurers but as agents who might unwittingly help discover the path to a universe far more cosmic than any that astronauts or the engineers who dispatched them had ever dreamed of. ★ They were interested in UFOs—flying saucers—to be sure. But to leave it at that is to consign them to the oatbin of history reserved for those who succumb, in the words of the title of Charles Mackay's famous book, to "extraordinary popular delusions and the madness of crowds." As you will sense immediately from Douglas Curran's own words and pictures, these people are in fact part of a religion. And that religion is, at bottom, not terribly different from most other new religions of the past two millennia. Most of them, the successful ones as well as those that have vanished, have been based on the belief that there exists Another Order, invisible to the great mass of humanity. It is this Other Order, and not merely the physical order of the physicists, astronomers, and economists, that determines the fate of man and creates the music of the spheres. The revelation of this Other Order has typically come from the sky. The flaming archangel of Ahura Mazda descends from above to speak to Zoroaster.... The heavens open and light shines upon Saul on the road to Damascus and a voice booms down: "Saul, Saul, why persecuteth thou me?" ... By the logic of these precedents, what could be more natural than to assume that today Another Order would be at least as technologically advanced as man here on earth and a good bit more inspired and ingenious in its heavenly revelations? ★ But it is not the visions of Douglas Curran's people that make them so compelling. It is the very tangible fabric of their lives, and anyone looking at his pictures will *feel* it immediately. It is in this wholly mundane sphere that you are likely to be struck by Douglas Curran's ability as a reporter and as an artist. We never see the Other Order that his subjects search for. Instead, we see something considerably more moving: their struggle to rise above the plain facts of their lives here on earth. In most cases those facts are very plain indeed, and they engage our attention more poignantly than anything in the heavens above. ★ Douglas Curran's own long quest has been to record these earthly scenes. In his relentless focus on the look and feel of the here and now he deserves a place alongside Lewis Hine, Arnold Genthe, William McFarlane Notman, August Sander, and perhaps even Henry Mayhew, who pushed the reporting of unknown souls to the edge of brilliance in *London Labour and the London Poor*. **—Tom Wolfe**

Deus Ex Machina

In the fall of 1977 I bought a second-hand yellow Renault 16. I christened it "Giselle," pulled out the rear seat, and fitted a small cupboard-desk in the space behind the driver's seat. The passenger seat folded down into a bed at night, and with the glove compartment open I was able to find room for my feet. With more a hunch than a plan, I began driving, looking for objects that people might have made to express their ideas about outer space and the future. I followed secondary highways through towns and cities, from British Columbia down the West Coast, eventually circumscribing the United States along a counterclockwise route. Three months and 22,000 miles later I arrived in Toronto with a rough collection of negatives that became the basis of this book.

By the fall of 1978 I was on the road again, better equipped with a 4×5 camera and an emerging awareness of a new mythology of gods and technology as relevant to twentieth-century civilization as Zeus and Apollo had been to the ancient Greeks. Giselle was my home for months at a time for several years. I might wake up in Ontario one morning and not shut the engine off until Kansas, on my way to a flying-saucer convention. I lost track of the miles. One day the speedometer needle fell off, and I was delighted to see the end of its nagging.

Initially I sought information about backyard rockets and flying saucers from newspaper editors, waitresses, and gas station attendants in the towns and cities I drove through. I would fan out postcards made from some photographs taken during my first trip and say: "I'm studying what people think about outer space. Have you seen anything around here that looks like this?" Many times the discussion that followed would involve the whole newsroom or café in a debate over the possibilities of life on other planets and alien visitations to Earth. Eventually much information for the project was to come from an expanding circle of UFO researchers, science fiction buffs, and sociologists, but luck and driving—the turn of the steering wheel like a roll of the dice—uncovered more than any single researcher.

The title, *In Advance of the Landing: Folk Concepts of Outer Space,* had come to me, full blown, in the middle of a dream one night in 1975. I woke up, wrote the words down, and carried them with me in a notebook for two years without attaching any particular meaning to them.

It was while rounding a curve on a two-lane highway in Quebec that I found my first rocket. Thrust out over the trees lining the highway, it was held in simulated flight, reflecting the last light of the sun. Deus ex machina! The rocket seemed to strain against its metal pylons, a totem attempting to leap away from the gravity of Earth to the realms of the gods. It was at one and the same time the quintessential product of western civilization, a daydream of technology, and a symbol of transcendence and freedom. It was nostalgia for the future.

Charlie LaBranche's rocket.
South Bolton, Quebec.
It was Charlie LaBranche's rocket that
motivated me to begin work on *In Advance
of the Landing: Folk Concepts of Outer Space*.
LaBranche hired two local carpenters in
1964 to build the rocket to stand outside his
general store. The rocket has brought him years
of pleasure. As he says in his thick Québecois
accent, "I love to watch the cars come
around the corner and fall off the pavement."

The discovery of this roadside rocket galvanized that obscure phrase in my notebook, the fragments of ideas about myth and archetypes that I had begun gathering from the writings of Carl Jung, and my growing need to rechannel my photographic ambitions. Scraps of information previously ignored, from newspapers and chance conversations, began to form themselves into a shopping list for the project.

My intent was never to prove or disprove the existence of flying saucers or extraterrestrial beings. The difficulty I have sometimes experienced in communicating this fact is a function of the general confusion about UFOs, compounded by the public's seemingly insatiable appetite for any news about them. Near the end of most interviews the interviewer will lean toward me with a kind of "just-between-you-and-me" attitude, and I *know* that it is time for The Question. "So tell me, Doug," I am asked in a gentle and excessively familiar voice, "do you think UFOs really exist?"

According to 1978 and 1981 Gallup polls, a majority of the North American adult population believes in the existence of flying saucers controlled by intelligent beings from another planet. Outer space and flying saucers and aliens from other worlds, with all manner of attendant beliefs about their origins and purposes, are firmly rooted in contemporary popular culture. Evangelist Billy Graham has publicly stated that "UFOs are astonishingly angellike in some of their reported appearances." The dramatic finale of the 1984 Los Angeles Olympics, witnessed by 120 million Americans on their home television sets, was the descent of a huge flying saucer over the stadium.

Rocket along Highway 1.
Apache Junction, Arizona.

No one will know for sure if flying saucers exist until the discovery of physical evidence. And yet UFOs will not go away—sightings by reputable witnesses accumulate daily. After studying the UFO phenomenon through newspaper and U.S. Air Force reports, Carl Jung paraphrased Edward J. Ruppelt, the head of the Air Force's UFO investigation: "Something is seen, but one doesn't know what." As I got to know the personalities involved with the UFO phenomena, the edges of fact, conjecture, wishful thinking, and supernatural events began to overlap and blur. To begin to understand what UFOs mean to contemporary society, I had to unravel the convoluted and little-known sequence of events that led to the current beliefs about them. David M. Jacob's *The UFO Controversy in America* (1975) offered an enlightening and insightful guide to the lead players and their roles in this cosmic whodunit.

Mysteries have always appeared in the sky. Whether these are real objects, misapprehended natural phenomena, alien visitors, or angelic hosts, they have been seen and recorded throughout history. The Bible, for example, brings us the cryptic account of Ezekiel's Wheel (Ezekiel 10:10) and the tale of the Israelites being led by a cloud by day and a pillar of fire by night (Numbers 9:15). The ancient Romans wrote about seeing "phantom chariots" in the heavens. In 1566 Samuel Coccius, a student in Basel, reported that "many large black globes were seen in the air, moving before the sun at great

speed and turning against each other as if fighting. Some of them became red and fiery and afterwards faded and went out."

Closer to our own time was the Great Airship Mystery, which swept the United States in 1896 and 1897. Thousands of people across twenty states saw large cigar-shaped ships in the air, powered by motors that drove air screws, propellers, or wing-like sails. Witnesses emphatically denied that what they saw were conventional hot-air balloons or gliders. The April 10, 1897, issue of the *Chicago Tribune* carried a description of an airship that was seventy feet long, with twenty-foot wings or sails just above the body. In Dallas a ship was sighted "in a luminous hazy cloud" with "sails or wings outstretched on both sides of its cigar-shaped body."

Witnesses usually observed white or colored lights on the airships, and sometimes a white or red searchlight. In Benton Harbour, Michigan, a ship was seen with green, blue, and red lights. When a ship appeared over Everest, Kansas, at 9:05 p.m., the "full power of the wonderful lamps were turned on and the city was flooded with light." Thousands of spectators in Milwaukee watched as "the machine or whatever it was" hovered over the city hall and the lights on the airship moved back and forth across it "as if signaling to the earth." On other occasions ships were seen to be signaling to each other with colored lights. The airships were reported to be moving at speeds from five miles per hour to two hundred miles per hour. From some ships "sweet strains of music" could be heard, while other witnesses reported hearing the sounds of machinery and voices.

Some people had the opportunity to meet the pilots of the airships. In one case a number of citizens of Chattanooga, Tennessee, came across two men repairing their ship. John Barclay, a farmer in Rockland, Texas, lent tools to the "ordinary mortals" piloting a ship that had landed in a nearby pasture. The occupants wouldn't let Barclay inspect the ship, but before the airship took off "like a shot from a gun" they promised to return one day and give him a ride.

The most bizarre incident of the 1896–97 sightings, and one that presaged the 1970s rash of UFO cattle-mutilation cases, happened in Leroy, Kansas, on April 19, 1897. Alexander Hamilton, his son Wall, and a tenant were awakened by noise from their cattle yard. Going outside they found a cigar-shaped airship three hundred feet long with "panels of glass or other transparent substance, alternating with a narrow strip of some other material," descending over the cattle herd. Inside the ship, with its searchlights and small red and green lights, Hamilton could see "six of the strangest beings I ever saw." A red cable from the airship was fastened around a heifer. Hamilton and the other witnesses watched "in amazement to see ship, cow and all, rise slowly and sail off." The next day a neighbor discovered the calf's hide, legs, and head a few miles away. Newspapers that carried accounts of the incident printed affidavits from prominent local citizens who attested to Hamilton's reputation as an upstanding member of the community.

Thomas Edison declared the whole notion of airships to be absurd,

The Dynasoar rocket, along the
Trans-Canada Highway. Near Sussex,
New Brunswick.

but several other scientists did allow that "something unusual has been seen in the heavens." A number of hoaxes, including faked photographs, were foisted on the public, but these spurious incidents contrasted sharply with the stories by reliable witnesses, none of whom ever suggested that the airship occupants were other than human. Scientists of the time stated that it was impossible for the airships to be real, given the technology then available. Prominent astronomers explained that people were simply seeing the planet Venus or the stars of Alpha Orionis or Betelgeuse and that the atmosphere was creating the illusion of erratic movement and changing colors. (The fact that many of the airships had been seen on cloudy nights undermined these assertions.)

A variety of more imaginative theories about the origins of the airships were suggested. Some occupants of an airship that landed in Stephenville, Texas, told a group of witnesses, including a state senator, a judge, and the district attorney, that they were financed by New York "capitalists." While on a fishing trip, Judge Love of Waxachie, Texas, encountered an airship whose occupants stated that they were from a large unknown body of land beyond the northern polar seas, inhabited by the ten lost tribes of Israel. The *Chicago Tribune* said about one airship that the "vessel is purely a celestial body which has taken on a few terrestrial attributes in order to accommodate itself to the limitations of the human imagination." Other newspapers encouraged a theory of extraterrestrial origin for the ships, citing current ideas about Mars

with its "canals" and the popular science fiction of Jules Verne and H. G. Wells. The most logical explanation was the "secret inventor" theory, which held that the ships had been built by an anonymous inventor. By 1896 many patents had been granted for lighter-than-air craft, but it was not until 1900 that Leo Stevens built and flew a motor-powered dirigible. Given the varying descriptions of the ships and the distances involved, however, it seems unlikely that a single inventor, maintaining secrecy despite the nationwide publicity, could have accounted for all the airships.

The sightings faded out completely by the end of 1897, never satisfactorily explained. The public initially looked for rational explanations that would make sense given the known levels of science and technology. When these explanations proved unconvincing, a credibility gap grew between accepted knowledge and what had been seen. If man-made airships could not exist, then the witnesses who claimed to have seen them had obviously seen something else.

The modern interest in UFOs began in the last years of World War II. Allied aircraft crews became alarmed at the balls of light and disk-shaped objects that began to follow their aircraft as they flew over enemy territory. These balls of light were nicknamed "foo-fighters," after a *Smokey Stover* cartoon quip, "Where there's foo, there's fire." Foo-fighters would appear out of nowhere, pacing in front or back of the aircraft or dancing slowly alongside the wingtips. They never caused any damage, and Air Force intelligence thought that the balls of light were a secret psychological-warfare weapon. Only after the war was it discovered that Ger-

man and Japanese crews had experienced the same phenomenon and thought it was an Allied weapon. Navy personnel aboard ships also saw the foo-fighters, which they determined were not the electrical discharges known as St. Elmo's Fire. A U.S. Army study conducted after the war concluded that the foo-fighters were simply "mass hallucinations."

Kenneth Arnold's 1947 sighting of nine disk-shaped objects flipping around the summit of Mount Rainier, Washington, was the catalyst for American UFO studies. After his widely publicized report, sightings poured into newspapers, many of them predating Arnold's own. As with the Great Airship Mystery of 1896–97, initial news coverage was fair and impartial, but as the reports became more fantastic, the press turned to scorn and stressed the proven hoaxes. Kenneth Arnold, stung by the ridicule in the aftermath of his report, commented: "If I saw a ten-storey building flying through the air I would never say a word about it." Nonetheless, the sightings continued—over 850 in 1947 alone.

Again, as with the airships fifty years before, scientists, academics, and other professionals denied the very existence of such anomalous phenomena and concluded that witnesses had seen nothing at all. At the 1947 meeting of the American Association for the Advancement of Science, Dr. C. C. Wylie, an astronomer, suggested that the UFOs were an example of national hysteria encouraged by "the present failure of scien-

★

★

tific men to explain promptly and accurately flaming objects seen over several states, flying saucers and other celestial phenomena which arouse national interest." Other theories held that a "mild case of meteorological jitters" was responsible or a speeding plane that had churned up the atmosphere and thereby distorted light rays. The aviation pioneer Orville Wright was consulted about the mystery and declared that it had no scientific basis: "It is more propaganda for war to stir up the people and to excite them to believe a foreign power has designs on this nation."

A Gallup poll conducted in 1947 found that ninety per cent of the adult population were aware of flying saucers and that most thought the objects were illusions, hoaxes, secret weapons, or other explicable phenomena. Virtually no one considered the objects to be from outer space. Public interest in flying saucers remained high, and rumors began to circulate that they were caused by the atomic bomb. This prompted David Lilienthal, the chairman of the Atomic Energy Commission, to make a public statement discounting any connection between atomic bomb testing and the flying disks.

In 1947 the Air Force quietly began to compile flying-saucer reports, sending them to the Technical Intelligence Division of Air Materiel Command at Wright-Patterson Field in Dayton, Ohio. The public position of the Air Force on flying saucers was that they were misidentifications, but privately its greatest concern was that they were actually Russian secret weapons, built using technology developed by the Germans at the secret Peenemünde rocket works during World War II.

The Mantell incident of January 1948 drew more sensationalized press to the growing speculations about the origins of flying saucers. Witnesses in Louisville, Kentucky, observed a silvery, cone-shaped object, 300 feet in diameter and tipped with red, hovering over their city. The object was reported to state police, who contacted flight controllers at a nearby airbase. Captain Thomas Mantell, an Air National Guard pilot leading a group of P-51 fighters in the area, was asked to investigate. As he approached the object it sped away and continued climbing. Mantell notified the tower that he was going up after it. Obviously excited, he reported that the object was metallic and "tremendous in size." Without oxygen equipment Mantell lost consciousness at 20,000 feet, his plane went into a dive, and he crashed.

The fact that a person had died while chasing a flying saucer raised the possibility that they were not only extraterrestrial but hostile as well. The Air Force quickly issued a statement saying that Mantell had died while in pursuit of the planet Venus, having mistaken it for a UFO. The press and the public were incredulous at this explanation, which set the stage for an enduring theme in the UFO controversy: the Air Force is not telling all it knows.

The Mantell incident pressured the Air Force to solve the enigma of UFOs. The secret weapon theory was discounted by questioning former Peenemünde engineers such as Werner von Braun, and it also seemed improbable that Russians would conduct test flights of experimental craft over enemy territory. In addition, no known metals could endure the heat that would have been generated at the speeds reported by witnesses. The implications were unsettling: if the objects were neither Russian nor American, and if they performed beyond the capability of human devices, then perhaps they were not from Earth.

The UFO furor died down until July 1948, when another close encounter created headlines. Two pilots of a commercial DC-3 saw a cigar-shaped object with two rows of illuminated windows and a red-orange flame at one end traveling toward them at great speed. It streaked past the airliner at an estimated 700 miles per hour, made a sharp angular turn, climbed into a clear sky, and abruptly disappeared. Other people in the air and on the ground reported a bright light in the area at about the same time.

An Air Force group, called Project Sign, that was studying UFOs felt it was time to report their findings. Their "Estimate of the Situation," a position paper endorsing the extraterrestrial hypothesis, went through the chain of command to Chief of Staff General Hoyt S. Vandenburg, who declared that the report lacked proof and sent it back. Thereafter the staff supporting the theory of extraterrestrial visitation lost favor to those who felt that the flying saucers could be explained in conventional terms.

At the beginning of 1949 the Air Force reorganized both its UFO-investigating team and its procedures for dealing with UFO reports under the code name Project Grudge. The Air

★

Concrete flying saucer found in the
San Bernardino hills. Perris, California.

*

Force saw the project primarily as an exercise in public relations, rather than a serious effort to determine the origins of UFOs. The public relations aspect became even more critical after Russia produced its own atomic bomb later that year: with the cold war heating up, the Air Force felt that the appearance of flying saucers could create dangerous public confusion and even precipitate a Russian attack.

The Air Force lent considerable support and material to a two-part *Saturday Evening Post* article by Sidney Shallett in the April 30 and May 7, 1949, issues, attributing the sightings by pilots, among others, to "strange tricks" of the sun, stars, and senses. While admitting that some UFOs remained unidentified, the pieces dealt mainly with hoaxes and a number of easily explained sightings. The second article ended with a quote from a Nobel Prize–winning chemist, Dr. Irving Langmuir, advising the Air Force to "Forget it!" Response to the article was exactly the opposite of what the Air Force intended. A few days after the second installment appeared, UFO sightings hit an all-time high. The Air Force countered with a press release saying that the saucers were the result of national hysteria and misapprehended natural phenomena. The official denials motivated some people to begin studying UFOs on their own and eventually led to the establishment of a wide range of UFO groups across the country.

True magazine commissioned Donald E. Keyhoe, a retired Marine Corps major, to write an independently researched UFO article in late 1949. A pilot himself, Keyhoe had written several books and many magazine articles about aviation during the 1930s

15

and '40s, and he now turned to his colleagues in the upper echelons of the military for inside information. But Project Grudge wanted to quiet down the UFO brouhaha and refused to co-operate. To Keyhoe, the silence of his former confederates could mean only one thing: they had discovered that flying saucers came from outer space.

In "The Flying Saucers Are Real," published in *True* in January 1950, Keyhoe stated that "living, intelligent observers from another planet" had been scrutinizing Earth for the last 175 years. The visits had become more numerous in the past two years, he said, accounting for the sudden in-flux of reports. The article was a sen-sation, and that issue of *True* became the best selling in the magazine's his-tory. The public enthusiasm that it generated drowned out the Air Force's assertion that Keyhoe's article did not accurately reflect the facts. (Keyhoe expanded the piece into a book with the same title later in 1950.)

True followed "The Flying Saucers Are Real" with "How Scientists Tracked the Flying Saucers," in March 1950, by Navy Commander R. B. McLaughlin, a member of a team of scientists working at the White Sands missile proving grounds in New Mexico. McLaughlin recounted how scientists had sighted a silvery object while tracking a high-altitude Skyhook balloon. Estimated to be forty feet wide and one hundred feet long, the object traveled at an altitude of fifty-six miles at a speed of 25,200 miles per hour. McLaughlin offered that the object "was a flying saucer, and further, that these discs are spaceships from another planet."

With the publication, also in 1950, of Frank Scully's best-seller, *Behind the Flying Saucers,* a new element of flying-saucer lore appeared: the cap-tured alien. Reviewed in *Time, Satur-day Review,* and *Science Digest,* Scully's was the first well-known American UFO book. In it, Scully told a story originally related by Silas Newton, a Texas oilman, about "Dr. Gee," who had been approached by the Air Force to conduct a secret au-topsy on sixteen dead aliens that had been recovered from three crashed saucers. The aliens, it was purported, were about four feet tall, drank water twice as heavy as that on Earth, and had no cavities in their teeth; the metal of their spaceship was harder than any on this planet. (The specter of diminutive aliens with superhuman characteristics and resources was to become firmly rooted in contemporary culture.) The Dr. Gee story was later shown to be a hoax, and Newton and Mr. GeBauer ("Dr. Gee") were arrest-ed on a fraud charge several years later for attempting to sell a piece of war-surplus equipment as an oil-dowser.

The Air Force created its own public relations sensation in 1951 with articles in several national magazines that linked some flying-saucer reports with secret military projects and dis-missed others as the mental aberra-tions of "screwballs," "true believ-ers," and victims of "cold war jitters." For the time being, the battle for the hearts and minds of the public seemed to have been won by the Air Force: sightings for the first six months of 1951 totaled only seven-teen, and the Air Force began to dis-mantle Project Grudge. Then, several daytime sightings involving military pilots and radar contacts caught the Air Force off guard in late 1951, and a new investigation team was set up

under the code name Project Blue-book. The reports compiled by this group became classified documents, unavailable to the public until 1969, when the Air Force ended its investi-gation of UFO cases, twenty per cent of which they labeled "unknown" in origin.

Life magazine published "Have We Visitors from Outer Space?" by Robert Ginna and H. B. Darrach, in its April 7, 1952, issue. The staff of Proj-ect Bluebook had declassified sight-ing reports at the request of the writ-ers, who had the support of the Pentagon, and the article generated as much excitement as Keyhoe's piece had two years earlier. The writ-ers noted that the Air Force had de-termined that the disks, cylinders, and other geometric forms seen in the sky were not the weapons of a foreign power. The official Air Force explana-tions involving Skyhook balloons, psy-chological aberrations, and atomic-testing effects were ruled out by the authors in a number of detailed re-ports. "These objects," the authors insisted, "cannot be explained by present science as natural phenome-na—but solely as artificial devices created and operated by a high intel-ligence." In further support of their extraterrestrial interpretation, the article's authors quoted Dr. Walter Reidel, a former chief designer and research director of rockets at Pee-nemünde. Reidel stated that Earth materials would burn up from the fric-tion caused by the UFOs' reported maneuvers and that no human pilot could withstand the resulting centrifu-gal forces. The absence of jets or va-por trails indicated an unknown source of power. "I am completely convinced," Reidel concluded, "that they have an out-of-world basis."

Flying Saucer Gas Bar. Lloydminster,
Saskatchewan.

The *Life* article concluded with a list of questions: "What power urges them at such terrible speeds through the sky? Who, or what is aboard? Where do they come from? Why are they here? What are the intentions of the beings who control them?

"Before these awesome questions, science—and mankind—can yet only halt in wonder. Answers may come in a generation—or tomorrow. Somewhere in the dark skies there may be those who know."

The UFO controversy boiled down to two main points of view: either flying saucers existed or they did not. The Air Force believed that the phenomenon, as a source of confusion, represented a threat to national security and could be explained in prosaic terms. The opposing view, that flying saucers represented a unique phenomenon that defied established conventions of science and technology, was held by the newly formed civilian investigation groups such as the Aerial Phenomena Research Organization (APRO) of Wisconsin and Civilian Saucer Investigation of Los Angeles. From the scientific community perhaps only Dr. J. Allen Hynek, an astronomer from Northwestern University and consultant to Projects Sign and Bluebook, supported the extraterrestrial hypothesis.

The ongoing debate was distorted by the appearance of the flying-saucer "contactees," who claimed to have experienced face-to-face—or, at least, mind-to-mind—contact with the intelligences controlling the saucers. While the Air Force and other civilian groups struggled to present proof to support their opposing positions, the contactees simply sidestepped the entire debate, offering instead the ready answers that so many people

"The Rocketman," built in 1959 to commemorate John Glenn's flight. Houston, Texas.

★

craved. For the Air Force, the contactees were a mixed blessing: they tended to discredit the subject in the eyes of the public and the scientific community, but at the same time they were tremendously effective at garnering headlines. The ridicule heaped upon the contactees' outrageous claims and hoaxes hindered the efforts of serious civilian investigators to present their own less dramatic findings.

Contactees such as George Adamski, Orfeo Angelucci, Truman Bethurum, Howard Menger, and Daniel Fry were in the media spotlight throughout the 1950s and into the '60s. In their 1957 book, *Flying Saucer Pilgrimage,* Bryant and Helen Reeve painted broad and enthusiastic portraits of all the major and many of the minor space communicants of the period, whom they encountered during a 23,000-mile journey across America. In contrast to the reluctance with which most UFO witnesses related their experiences, if they did so at all, the contactees were known for their confident way of presenting themselves and their information. The Reeves wrote admiringly about a 1954 press conference with George Adamski in Detroit, where "The questioning and photographing lasted several hours. Mr. Adamski was standing up under the barrage. He was doing more than that; he was gradually creating a miracle, a lessening of skepticism and an increase of respect!" This triumph was repeated at a radio station, where "An unusual feeling of sincerity was sensed. A thrill stole over the broadcast room. Technicians and helpers paused in their work to listen—almost in awe—to this simple man who told of his contact . . . with a man from another world."

The contactees spoke eagerly about the wondrous beings they had met and the messages they had been ordained to deliver to humanity. While conversing with a "Master" on board a spaceship, Adamski was informed that Earth presented two problems for the other planets in the galaxy: how to save the Earth from its own nuclear destruction and how to save the universe from Earth. Orfeo Angelucci was told by a space contact that Earth, the "home of sorrows," would undergo a "Great Accident" in 1986 if humanity did not learn to work together for the common good. At another time, Jesus told him that space people were everywhere on Earth, in disguise, helping the human race.

A flying saucer landed near Daniel Fry one night at the White Sands Missile Range. "Better not touch the hull, pal, it's still hot," a voice warned as Fry approached the ship. The voice belonged to A-lan, who informed him that Earthlings were dangerously "out of balance" because our physical sciences had progressed far ahead of our religious and social sciences. The problem, A-lan explained, could only be solved by countries and individuals *understanding* one another, and so Fry formulated a number of "Understanding Inc." study groups all across the country.

As the demand for further communications increased, both from spiritualist groups and the general public, the contactees were pressured to elaborate on their experiences. The spiritual message brought by the contactees gradually became more sophisticated, dressed in the intricate jargon and ritual of mystic societies. Adamski, for example, resurrected a metaphysical tract that he had written in the 1930s by substituting "the Space Brothers" for "the Royal Order of Tibet" throughout the text.

Roland Choquette at his gas station.
North of Winnipeg, Manitoba.

Several harbingers of the new cosmic order—including George King and the Aetherius Society, Mark Probert and his Inner Circle, and Ernest L. and Ruth Norman and their Unarius Foundation—had previously been engaged in metaphysical studies, and they derived many of their ideas from Helena Blavatsky's Theosophy movement. This richly textured and widely influential religion, begun in the 1870s, espoused reincarnation and offered spiritual guidance through direct contact with a hierarchy of masters, or "Mahatmas," known as the "Great White Brotherhood." A Theosophist community established in San Diego in 1899 evolved its own heroic architecture, schools, musical and dramatic troupes, and agricultural programs. Offshoots of Theosophy revealed themselves in popular 1930s movements such as Guy Ballard's I AM, Rudolf Steiner's Anthroposophy, and the Rosicrucian Fellowship. Each of the 1950s groups transformed certain fixtures of Theosophy to create a seemingly new belief system, which helped attract those already involved in spiritualism. Adding flying saucers to the cosmic plan and expanding the Great White Brotherhood to include extraterrestrial masters known as the Space Brothers gave the traditional Theosophical beliefs a contemporary relevance.

At conventions across the country an eager public gathered to learn the truth about flying saucers. George Van Tassel's first Interplanetary Spacecraft Convention, held in 1954 at Giant Rock, California, attracted over 5,000 people and extensive media coverage. Gabriel Green's Amalgamated Flying Saucer Clubs of America attracted thousands to its Los Angeles conventions in the late 1950s, which would feature over forty-five speakers during the two-day event. Edna Spencer, a twenty-five-year member of the Aetherius Society, recalled that when she first met George King in Detroit in 1959: "It was amazing, it was like a fever! . . . back at that time flying saucers were *brand new* and there weren't all these movies on flying saucers around. It amazes me to realize that there's a generation who grew up with that—they don't know anything different."

The degree to which the mythology of the flying saucer has been integrated into contemporary culture can be illustrated by comparing the 1951 film *The Day the Earth Stood Still* with Steven Spielberg's 1977 production, *Close Encounters of the Third Kind*. In the former, a handsome, benevolent being from a utopian planet lands his flying saucer near the White House to bring the message to Earthlings that atomic testing is harming other planets. Reacting with fear and hostility, the people of Earth attempt to destroy him. The alien escapes, mingles with the populace, and eventually is able to relay his message to top scientists. Steven Spielberg, a member of the baby boom generation who grew up with flying saucers, conceived his 1977 classic differently, with humanity eagerly anticipating the visit from outer space. The alien ship of *Close Encounters* descends in a blaze of light that suggests the second coming of Christ. "The UFO phenomenon is the most seductive and significant adventure into the unknown of our lifetime," Spielberg ventures, thereby casting a pall over such other accomplishments as decoding the DNA molecule, photographing quasars at the edge of the universe, and human excursions to the moon.

Coincidental with the arrival of Spielberg's film was the departure of two Voyager spacecraft, the first Earth vehicles flung out of our solar system to wander in the galaxy. Included as part of their cargo were images of animals, houses, people, and families as well as music selections from Bach to Chuck Berry and greetings in fifty-five languages, recorded on a twelve-inch copper disk.

The *Newsweek* cover story of November 21, 1977, was "The UFOs Are Coming." In it, Dr. J. Allen Hynek, long-suffering in his attempts to bring scientific standards to UFO-investigation, was at last vindicated and dubbed "The Galileo of UFOlogy." In a 1982 conversation at his Chicago home, Hynek talked about the frustrations he had encountered in trying to study UFOs seriously. Despite the *Newsweek* article and the success of *Close Encounters*—whose title had been his own creation—the necessary funds for research had still not materialized. The enigma to which he had dedicated his career remained inscrutable and unacceptable to the scientific community. Hynek submitted that perhaps UFOs were part of a parallel reality, slipping in and out of sequence with our own. This was a hypothesis that obviously pained him as an empirical scientist. Yet after thirty years of interviewing witnesses and investigating sighting reports, radar contacts, and physical traces of saucer landings no other hypothesis seemed to make sense to him.

Flying Saucer Drive-in.
Niagara Falls, Ontario.
Henry DiCienzo built the Flying Saucer Drive-in in 1972 with the help of his father. The concrete and wire-lath structure has been recently enlarged and now boasts ninety-six lights around its rim. DiCienzo says of his lifelong fascination with flying saucers: "I'd like to see one. I believe they're there."

Flying Saucer Gift Shop, built in 1972.
Cavendish, Prince Edward Island.

Although centered primarily in North America, the UFO phenomenon is universal, with sightings being reported from the steppes of Russia to the South African veldt. The belief in flying saucers as messengers of divine goodwill is equally widespread; in Yokohama, Japan, a large white saucer dominates a peace park hillside, and in the barrios of Rio de Janeiro crudely painted UFOs decorate tin shacks. Although the details vary, descriptions of the form and behavior of UFOs are nearly identical throughout the world. While UFOs may not have a physical existence, there can be no doubt that they have a psychological one, fulfilling a deep need in the human psyche. In his 1957 essay on flying saucers, Jung wrote: "In the threatening situation of the world today, when people are beginning to see that everything is at stake, the projection-creating fantasy soars beyond the realm of earthly organizations and powers into the heavens, into interstellar space, where the rulers of human fate, the gods, once had their abode in the planets."

In the years since Jung wrote his essay a number of world events have proven to be psychologically destabilizing, particularly for Americans: Sputnik, Vietnam, Watergate, the Arab oil embargo. Overshadowing everything is the global consciousness that we are in danger of destroying human life on Earth with nuclear weapons. The fears of atomic war communicated by the alien Orthon to George Adamski in 1952 are echoed in the statements of Ann Magnuson, a New York artist, in 1981: "Now I just think about being bombed everyday.... Who wants to survive? I want to stand out in the street and get it full

force. Our only hope is the space people. I really want them to come save us."

As popularly conceived, the flying saucer is a god wrapped in stainless steel. As a technological construction, it exceeds objects of our own manufacture. Its smooth continuous form is without the defects that mark objects on Earth: seams, discontinuity of surface, angularity. In flight it surpasses the capabilities of earthbound devices, hovering and zigzagging in a manner that suggests weightlessness. Like a god, it seems to be everywhere and nowhere at the same time.

For Jung the saucer represented an archetype of order, wholeness, deliverance, and salvation—a symbol manifested in other cultures as a mandala, sun wheel, or magic circle. It was left to our industrialized culture to integrate this mythological archetype into a new technological form. "Anything that looks technological," Jung noted, "goes down without difficulty with modern man." The Space Brothers aboard the flying saucers bring a timeless hope of salvation, much as angelic messengers did in earlier times. The spiritual message they convey is recognizably our own—they do not advocate any moral or metaphysical belief that is not firmly rooted in Judeo-Christian tradition. (Every single flying-saucer group I encountered in my travels incorporated Jesus Christ into the hierarchy of its belief system.)

Beliefs—especially those dealing with the nature of man and the structure of the cosmos—need not be true in an ultimate sense to be psychologically real and socially functional. Sociologists acknowledge this in their work with groups: a belief is true if it is seen to be true by those believing in it. We often employ the word *myth* to connote a fable or false story. But

in its traditional sense, myth is a narration of how in primordial time, through the deeds of gods or supernatural beings, a new reality came into being. The myth always relates a story that is sacred, exemplary, and significantly tied to human experience. Our most sacred beliefs-myths—those that express our understanding of the Other, God, or the Unknown—are ones that are codified in idea and rite as religion. As such, religion does not so much constitute objective truths about the universe as subjective statements about humanity's hopes and fears. Through religious beliefs an individual deals with the *unknown*. Religion-myth becomes a Rorschach figure onto which each person's anxieties are projected. New myths are called into being when the circumstances of the world change and challenge the prevalent beliefs or myths.

On my travels across the continent I never had to wait too long for someone to tell me about his or her UFO experience, whether I was chatting with a farmer in Kansas, Ruth Norman at the Unarius Foundation, or a café owner in Florida. What continually struck me in talking with these people was how positive and ultimately life-giving a force was their belief in outer space. Their belief reaffirmed the essential fact of human existence: the need for order and hope. It is this that establishes them—and me—in the continuity of human experience. It brought me to a greater understanding of Oscar Wilde's observation, "We are all lying in the gutter—but some of us are looking at the stars."

★

"Well, this thing with rockets is real good.... Man's divine y'know! Didn't used to be though. Had to be some of those extraterrestrials come down from Heaven and mated with the bare-assed baboons and made man. So we just got to get a *bigger* rocket— get back to where we came from."

Roadside conversation,
Kansas, Highway 54

★

In Advance of the Landing

Ruth Norman heads the Unarius Educational Foundation, preparing Earth
for the arrival of spaceships from the
Intergalactic Confederation. El Cajon,
California.

The Unarius Foundation presents members with a complete and ordered cosmography. Earth, they believe, is "the garbage dump of the universe," the place where unfulfilled souls end up until they achieve enough of a karmic bank balance to bail themselves out. Our planet operates at such a low level of consciousness that it even *vibrates* at a low frequency. To raise that consciousness, to increase that frequency, is the goal of the Unariuns. Such a move, they believe, would send a cosmic "yes" to the Intergalactic Confederation. Thirty-two spaceships—one from each planet of the Intergalactic Confederation—would then "land on Planet Earth to help this rapidly dying world . . . to teach mankind a better, a higher and happier way of life. . . ."

The power for such an ambitious endeavor comes from an eighty-two-year-old widow, Ruth Norman. Unariuns know her as the Archangel Uriel, the present incarnation of a supreme spiritual being who has visited Earth many times before. I first spoke to her on the telephone from Albuquerque. "You must be a very intelligent person, obviously, to be doing this kind of work," she said. "You're a caring person—I can tell by your voice. But I can also tell by the speech impediment and hesitancy in your voice that you were the captain of a pirate spaceship back at the time of the last civil war in the Orion Nebula and responsible for destroying hundreds of thousands of innocent lives. Your speech impediment and your present work on this planet are

proof of your karmatic starvation and your need to come to terms with your past lives. I suggest you undergo Unarius training. We can send some books out to you at a very reasonable cost." (While most of my friends would agree that I have an unusual way of enunciating, no one had ever leveled "speech impediment" at me before.) We talked for an hour, Ruth speaking about unfulfilled souls, the mission of Unarius on Earth, and how the fleet of ships from the Space Brothers would land here once they stopped receiving the tremendous psychic negations emitted by Earthlings of low consciousness.

Several weeks later I arrived at Unarius headquarters in El Cajon, California, and was interrogated by Uriel's lieutenant, a pale, round-faced, balding man with woebegone blue eyes. He had originally been named Vaughn Spaegel, but since a "past-life reading" had revealed that he had once been Charlemagne, he would now answer only to Charles. Satisfied about my identity and my intentions, he phoned Uriel. She agreed to come over shortly to meet me.

In preparation for Uriel's arrival, the group members spruced themselves up and lined up from the street curb to the front door. Suddenly, an electric blue '73 Cadillac with a glowing plexiglass-and-Mylar saucer on its roof wheels around the corner onto South Magnolia. Out steps Uriel, with rhinestone flecks on her eyelids, hair the color of orange sherbet, and a flowing purple chiffon gown. Students kiss her hand and bestow faintly acknowledged greetings. Her eyes cruise over the small crowd, and she makes a grand gesture with the folds

of her gown, asking, with just a hint of annoyance in her voice, "Where do you want me to stand?"

Displayed at the Unarius headquarters is a large fold-out tableau of color photographs depicting the twenty-six past Earth lives of Uriel: Ruth Norman is portrayed in full period costume as Confucius, Socrates, Henry VIII, and even Benjamin Franklin. She is also said to have lived among the higher-consciousness peoples of the thirty-two worlds of the Intergalactic Confederation, planets such as Vidis, Janus, and Vulna. Hundreds of thousands of years ago, the battling factions of the civil war that wracked the Orion Nebula successfully resolved themselves into the Confederation. Through the many lives these people have had, and the saving graces of such higher beings as Uriel, they have since attained a higher state, free of war, poverty, mental illness, disease, pollution, and energy problems. The only way for Earthlings to reach such an elevated level is to follow Unariun teachings and to gradually counter accumulated past negations through awareness of them. The process may take many lifetimes, but one will eventually be capable of helping others, as Uriel does now.

The Unarius headquarters is located in a commercial building sandwiched between the Salvation Army store and the county court buildings in downtown El Cajon. Large plate-glass windows across the front of the building display hardbound copies of Unariun publications and several of Uriel's radiant gowns. Visitors entering the headquarters are met by the cooing of caged doves; garlands of rhododendron and philodendron trail along the valance. Everything is in shades of light blue and capped with a Roman fresco motif. Large plaster statues, bouquets of flowers, and ornate tile-topped tables give a sense of sumptuous antiquity. Faint lilting chords of harp and violin, a celestial Muzak from hidden speakers, suggest the music of Heaven. Everything combines to make headquarters seem like a garden, a paradise, ethereal.

On the walls are paintings by Unariun artists: the "Wheel of Continuity," charts of Heaven and Hell, people being dragged into darkness and oblivion, people following the ways of the angels. All the archangels in the paintings have the face of a young Ruth Norman. One of the largest canvases is of Ioshanna, the Healing Princess of Light, a beatific bride-of-tomorrow in a long white bridal gown and a blonde bouffant hairstyle reminiscent of the early 1960s, with circles of healing light emanating from her eyes (unmistakably Ruth's), her forehead, her outstretched palms.

One of the Unariun students I stayed with, Dan Smith, stars as Zan the Hunter in an elaborate Unariun-produced film, *The Arrival.* Zan, a Stone Age hunter on Earth, first appears in a loincloth, dirty, with several days of beard growth, though still sporting his usual tidy haircut. Suddenly, a light from above splits the landscape and draws him to a beautiful crystalline spaceship, a shimmering saucer with glowing amber legs and a rim of pulsing ruby. From the belly of the ship appear a shaft of light and a bald-headed sage, who says, "Zan, do not be afraid."

"Me, Zan, me fearless hunter for my people," Dan replies.

The Space Brothers—wan creatures with pancaked faces, lightning bolts on their cheeks, and silver Mylar uniforms—explain to Zan that in one of his past lives he had been a leader who betrayed his people for riches and glory. In another, he had been a pirate captain who ordered the destruction of an innocent planet. Through dramatized flashbacks, Zan learns about his various other past lives, comes to terms with them, and becomes a new and higher-consciousness person. Everybody in the Unariun pantheon was, at some time or another, a conspirator, a corrupt prince or princess—a regal, powerful personage whose actions imperiled whole worlds and millions of lives. No one was a shoemaker who shortchanged a customer.

The acknowledgment of amassed guilt from past lives is the first part of the healing-enlightenment process. These explorations of the past tend to revolve around Uriel. A student might come to a reading session, as one related to me, and reveal, "I had a dream, a realization of my life on the planet Deva where I committed a terrible atrocity. I was a usurper of power. When the king came with Uriel to watch the pageant I blew up the stadium, not realizing in my ignorance that I couldn't truly kill Uriel." After group discussion of such a revelation, one of the senior teachers will correct any points that do not fit in with Unariun cosmological history. The past-life negation is then expunged, and the student is lifted to "a more regenerative position in his scale of life," moving toward that "psychic polarization and oscillation directed by the Perfected Minds on Higher Frequency Worlds." After one session, I watched strong men break into tears as they realized what they had done to Uriel in past lives and how kind she was just to let them appear in her presence now.

My first night there Ruth noticed me looking at a translucent lavender flying-saucer–shaped object with lights inside, hanging above the stage. "Oh that," she said, dismissing the object with a flick of her hand, "that's just a bit of a god symbol for the kiddies." She immediately seemed to regret her comment, becoming stiff and ill at ease.

Members are being carefully prepared for Ruth's death: Uriel may soon be going back with the Space Brothers to her place elsewhere in the universe. Arieson, the former Stephen Yancoskie of Erie, Pennsylvania, is her obvious heir apparent. Delays, unbelievers, false alarms do not deter Ruth. In a recent letter to Neosha Mandragos, a former Milwaukee nun turned Unariun, she writes, "Dear Neosha, I've been very busy the last few days. I've felt the Space Brothers were coming and I've been packing my bags. . . ."

★

Interior of Unarius headquarters, with a model depicting Ruth Norman's late husband, Ernest L. Norman, at his present job as Moderator of the Universe. El Cajon, California.
See page 32.

Landing site for the thirty-two city-
ships from the Intergalactic Confederation, near Jamul, California.
See page 33.

Among the rows of Unarius literature—with titles such as *The Little Red Box* (providing proof of Ernest L.'s past life as Jesus of Nazareth), *Have You Lived on Other Worlds Before?* (explaining the cosmic hierarchy and history of the Intergalactic Worlds), and *Who Is the Mona Lisa?* ("Through psychic attunement is discovered the long-sought answer to this question")—stands a model of Ruth Norman's late husband Ernest L., who departed this world in 1971, at work at his headquarters on Mars. From his ankh-shaped chrome chair, Ernest L., also known as Alta, presses jeweled buttons to communicate psychically with the thirty-two worlds of the Intergalactic Confederation and with Earth, which is a candidate to become number thirty-three. The screens that ring the wall above his head provide video images of whomever he wishes to contact, at any point in the universe. Vaughn Spaegel-Charles is his contact on Earth, and through him Ernest L. transmits up-to-date messages from the Confederation to the Unarius faithful.

During the early 1950s Ernest L., who was at that point a frail, unemployed "electronics engineer," operated in conjunction with two San Diego–area UFO-contact groups—Meade Layne's Borderland Sciences Research Associates and Mark Probert's followers of the Inner Circle—both of which borrowed heavily from Theosophy. It was while giving a lecture, "Inner Contact from the Higher Beings," in Los Angeles in 1954 that Ernest L. met Ruth. Together they formed the Unarius Educational Foundation, traveling the "book-and-trance" circuit of spiritualist conventions. During the seventeen years that Ernest L. and Ruth worked together, Unarius had neither a large membership nor any features to distinguish it from a number of other medium-spiritualist groups. The slight Ernest L. in his rumpled gray suit, with Ruth as the congenial and matronly hostess, conducted meetings and study sessions in rented halls and borrowed rec rooms. It was not until after the death of Ernest and the purchase of the headquarters building in 1974 that Ruth began to transform herself and Unarius, creating elaborate visual metaphors for the higher realms.

★

★

In 1967 the Space Brothers instructed Ruth Norman to prepare a landing site for the arrival of thirty-two city-ships from the Intergalactic Confederation. Ruth promptly bought sixty-seven acres of rolling hills near the rural community of Jamul, twenty miles east of San Diego. The irregular topography of the area would be no problem, Unariuns later explained to me: as the saucers land they will simply laser-blast the hills to create level ground.

In years past, generally around Christmas or Easter, Ruth-Uriel would receive notice from the Intergalactic Confederation that a landing was imminent. Unariuns, followed by jostling television crews, reporters, and photographers, would converge on the site to await the spacecraft. In 1975 Uriel, assured of the Arrival by the Brothers, led the Unariun faithful on an extravagantly produced all-night vigil, attended by action-hungry media. She subsequently filed a lawsuit against one of the television stations that aired a condemning broadcast of the event. Since then the Conclave of Light, a yearly convention and celebration of Unarius, has replaced the more unpredictable rites at the Jamul site. I asked Ruth why they had stopped meeting at the landing site. "*They* know we are here," she answered, "and that we're working. If they're coming then they'll come, but there's no point . . . we don't have to be there. Our psychic vibrations reach them wherever they are."

The second annual convention, or Conclave of Light, in May 1981 drew over four hundred members from throughout California and as far as Milwaukee, Toronto, and New York. Like the Bond family, who are active members from El Toro, California, everyone dresses in costumes from their past lives on other planets. Kenneth Bond, a successful businessman, and his wife, Birgit, are bringing up their sons according to Unariun concepts. The boys, Derek and Stephen, report that they find a great deal of acceptance for Unariun ideas among their friends at high school.

The Conclave opens with a procession. Arieson, dressed in the purple fringed toga of a Roman emperor, with a circlet of gilded olive leaves around his head, stands on stage to give the signal for the procession to begin. Accompanied by the rising strains of Ravel's *Bolero,* two girls dressed as peacocks in green Danskins and feather tail-pieces, with a man leading them by golden chains fastened around their necks, execute a dance adapted from a Busby Berkeley musical as they move up the center aisle. They are followed by two nymphs in pale turquoise chiffon and small gold tiaras strewing rose petals from cornucopias; a man wearing a white-feathered bird's head and long cloak carrying two doves in a gilded cage; and three sages, the first a Diogenes with a lamp, the second bearing the large Unarius Book of Life, and the third holding the symbolic Light of Healing.

People in costume parade banners emblazoned with the names of the thirty-two worlds of the Intergalactic Confederation. Everyone is doing a lilting march as *Bolero* builds toward its crescendo. Last of all comes Uriel, in a plumed palanquin adorned with large, feathery white swans, borne by four Nubian slaves, muscular fellows wearing skin-bronzer, headdresses, loincloths, and gilded beach thongs. She is unleashed onstage brandishing a sparkly wand with a sunburst of reflective Mylar at the end, nodding and blessing the crowd until the music wails down and everyone is welcomed to the day's proceedings.

All of this is sandwiched between a gathering of salesmen and a local teachers' conference in the Town and Country Convention Center, a Muzak-permeated suburban complex. Everywhere, amid pamphlet-laden tables and models of spaceship interiors and "New Age" science experiments, Unariuns are wandering in their heavy makeup, their ruby and emerald and sapphire metallic costumes.

There are moments of high emotion. After a slide presentation about life on several of the Confederation planets and a film from Mars, a short film drama entitled *The Cosmic Generator* is shown. Uriel, being the infinite spirit of the universe, is the "Cosmic Generator." She wears a black velvet gown plumped with crinolines to stand eight feet wide at the hem and surmounted by a collar decorated with flame appliqués fanning out in a huge semicircle behind her

head. In the middle of the bodice is the fiery Infinite Mind, a glowing hemisphere stuck onto the velvet. Rubber balls, painted yellow and pink and blue to represent the seas and continents of the Confederation worlds, spiral out to the edge of the skirt. The gown, the pointed golden "vortex" headdress, and the translucent elbow-length gloves with rapier nails have tiny light bulbs snaked through the fabric. Uriel glides down a sloping runway toward the audience and extends her arms. The bulbs explode into volleys of winking and blinking. Waves of light roll from bodice to fingertips, from Infinite Mind to planets. Strobes and multicolored lights flash as she kisses out from the screen, her beckoning gestures a pantomime of the Love and Light of Infinite Creation. A siren, she entices the audience to move past the void of guilt and unrecognized past lives and cross over the threshold of the Unariun universe. At that point, initiates fall off their chairs onto their knees and weep on the floor. The house lights are killed. Sobbing fills the auditorium as the lights are brought up again, slowly.

The Bond family at the Unarius Conclave of Light, wearing costumes from their past lives on other planets. San Diego, California.

The Warfield brothers, Brian and
Mike, at the Unarius Conclave of
Light. San Diego, California.

Brian and Mike Warfield help carry Uriel's palanquin during the opening procession of the Conclave of Light. Brian had been led to Unarius while attending college in Thousand Oaks, California, studying astronomy and philosophy. "I had read two or three metaphysical books, about life after death," explained Brian. "Then this one fellow told me about Unarius and who the Moderator is. That's what makes the difference of Unarius compared to any other metaphysical religion, you know.... Ernest L. was Raphael. Raphael was Jesus of Nazareth. Then I realized who Uriel is, and the fact that she was his wife is what gave me the faith and desire to want to be her student." Brian, along with Mike and his sister-in-law, Loretta, spoke of his seven-year involvement with Unarius as having exerted a positive influence on his life and goals. "All the psychic type of things, uncovering five major past lives, will be with me all my life.... Unarius gave me an attitude about not having limitations."

Other members—white and generally middle-class, like the Warfields—maintain outwardly conventional lives, though they tend to keep outside commitments to a minimum in order to spend as much time as possible at the foundation. I stayed with two Unarius students while photographing: Dan, who worked as assistant manager of an ice cream parlor, and George, who worked in a shoe store. They owned no more than the bare necessities, not even a car. Their sparsely furnished apartment was a transit station for ascending souls,

more camped-in than lived-in: the refrigerator offered only a carton of milk and an opened package of hot dogs. George and Dan had cassette tape machines at their bedsides and would get up listening to Unariun teachings. When taking a shower they simply turned up the volume. Tapes ran at a low murmur throughout the night.

Another Unarius member I met, Neosha Mandragos, lives in Milwaukee, where she had been a nun for twenty-seven years until she left the convent with fifty dollars and a cardboard suitcase. A year later she joined Unarius. Now a fifty-nine-year-old woman in rather poor health, she supports herself by baby-sitting and housecleaning in her working-class neighborhood. One room of her small, second-storey apartment is completely filled with Unarius pamphlets and wall hangings, as well as flying-saucer photographs from magazines, pictures of the space shuttle Columbia, anything about outer space. Neosha has an untiring devotion to Unarius and travels to California every year for the Conclave. As she sorted through the racks of costumes in preparation for the procession opening the Conclave, I overheard her sigh, "I'm tired of being a princess or a queen all the time. For a change I'd just like to be someone ordinary."

Mother Teresa at the St. Paul UFO
Landing Pad. St. Paul, Alberta.

A predominantly French-speaking rural community of 7,500 in north-central Alberta, St. Paul prides itself on its heritage and its public spirit. St. Paul also takes pride in possessing the world's first UFO landing pad, and signs along the highways leading into town boast of this fact.

The landing pad was built in 1967 as the town's project commemorating the Canadian Centennial. A sign at the foot of the stairs leading up to the pad declares:

> The area under the world's first UFO Landing Pad was designated international by the town of St. Paul as a symbol of our faith that mankind will maintain the outer universe free from national wars and strife. That future travel in space will be safe for all intergalactic beings. All visitors from Earth or otherwise are welcome to this territory and to the town of St. Paul.

Civic functions and all official welcoming ceremonies for visiting dignitaries, from rock stars to the prime minister, are conducted at the landing pad, which is tucked in a corner of a municipal lot on Main Street that also harbors a ball diamond and skating rink.

In 1982 the citizens of St. Paul decided to mark the International Year of the Child by aiding the missions of Mother Teresa in Calcutta. A large duplex constructed with donated labor and materials was put up for bidding, and the resulting funds were matched by the provincial and federal branches of government. On June 25, 1982, Mother Teresa arrived to be presented with the proceeds: $975,000. The tiny nun was driven down Main Street in a cavalcade of Jeeps with chrome rollbars and fog lamps. A high school band played as two sergeants-at-arms in white plumed hats and several Indians dressed in buckskins and feather headdresses greeted her on top of the landing pad.

The next two and a half hours were taken up by speeches from the politicians. When it came her turn to speak, Mother Teresa simply mentioned how fitting it was that a project of this type be celebrated at the landing pad and that "If there is sickness in outer space we would go there too." When she finished saying this she smiled and looked out over the crowd. Everyone clapped.

★

Clayton Bailey's "Alien Rocket."
Port Costa, California.
Clayton Bailey's major projects are
constructing robots with transplanted
brains and augmenting his fleet of 1947–49
Studebaker "rocket cars," which he
considers the last North American vehicles
to have "the true Look of the Future."
His "Alien Rocket" is based on the rep-
resentations of alien spacecraft that
were current before the "flying-saucer"
concept came into vogue in the 1950s.

*

Verdun Baxandahl's rocket.
Barrhead, Alberta.
Verdun Baxandahl and his son
constructed their twelve-foot rocket
from sheet aluminum and tin signs in
1958, shortly after Sputnik went up.
His reason for building the rocket was
simple: "Everyone was talking about
rockets and I wanted one."

Madeleine Rodeffer with model of an
Adamski saucer and a still photograph
from the 1965 "Silver Spring" film.
Silver Spring, Maryland.

Madeleine Rodeffer became interested in flying saucers through reading a 1954 classic about alien contact, Cedric Allingham's *Flying Saucers from Mars*. The book mentioned George Adamski's similar encounter with a blond Venusian named Orthon. A search of her local library turned up three titles by Adamski: *Flying Saucers Have Landed* (1953), *Inside the Space Ships* (1955), and *Flying Saucers Farewell* (1961). Deeply moved by Adamski's writings, Madeleine placed a call to his home near Mount Palomar, California. "I became so convinced that Mr. Adamski was telling the truth that the first time I called him on the phone, I offered, 'I would like to know what I can do to help you spread the word.'" Adamski's reply was simple and direct: "Read and learn all you can. Be open-minded and do what you feel is right."

"From that point on I thought, 'Well, if there's something out there worth looking at, I should look up too.'" Madeleine began searching out other UFO reports in the Washington, D.C., area through newspapers, radio, and television news departments. She made a trip to the Naval Observatory to learn the trajectories of satellites so that she would not mistake them for UFOs. At night she began to watch the skies with a pair of binoculars. "I felt that anyone from the sky—from other than Earth—was from Heaven," Madeleine stated. "Anyone coming here from Heaven in advanced spaceships would know more than we know here on Earth about life and life's purposes."

Although George Adamski was not the first person to claim contact with alien beings, his story was the first to attract widespread public attention. He had entered the United States at Ellis Island in 1892, at the age of one, with his Polish immigrant parents. The facts about his youth were never clear, even to his closest followers. When asked what he had done before settling in Mount Palomar, Adamski maintained that he had given popular lectures on astronomy and philosophy throughout New Mexico, Arizona, and California. He described himself as a wandering teacher, visiting settlements during the winter months when farmers had little to do and were pleased to see him. Fred Steckling, the current coordinator of the George Adamski Foundation, wrote in the *Cosmic Bulletin* of June 1979: "The qualification as a professor or teacher was given to him upon graduation from the highest school of Cosmic Law at a monastery in Tibet. This graduation was after an attendance of six years." Adamski privately claimed to have had contacts with extraterrestrials as a child and to have received instruction from them in Tibet.

The Federal Bureau of Investigation kept a file on George Adamski, for a number of reasons, and a declassified copy of this file gives a more exact account of his life. An agent's report of 1953 lists Adamski's occupations: from 1913 to 1916 he served with the U.S. Cavalry on the Mexican border and was honorably discharged; between 1916 and 1926 he was a painter and maintenance worker in Yellowstone National Park, a flour-mill worker in Portland, and a concrete contractor in Los Angeles. The entry for 1926 indicates that Adamski began to teach philosophy. During the 1930s he founded a monastery in Laguna Beach, dedicated to "The Royal Order of Tibet," and was given the title "Professor" by his students.

Throughout World War II, Adamski and his wife, Mary, helped run a small café owned by a friend and student, Alice Wells. The Mount Palomar Gardens was located at the foot of the road running up to the observatory at Mount Palomar. Adamski often held lectures on philosophy at the café, many times late into the night. People who met him there were invariably impressed by his warm, ingenuous manner and plain speech. He retained a slight accent throughout his life, unable to pronounce the sound "th."

The view from the Gardens sweeps westward to the coastal mountains and southward to San Diego and the Pacific Ocean. While watching a meteor shower from this vantage point in 1946, Adamski first sighted a large cigar-shaped spacecraft. Already an avid astronomer, he began spending all his available time outdoors, looking at the sky, stars, and moon. He began to see more indications of the mysterious ships: sometimes as they crossed the face of the moon, sometimes as sudden brilliant flashes of light during the day or night, and sometimes as lights zipping off at erratic angles impossible for conventional aircraft.

Adamski claimed that in 1949 two men from the Naval Electronics Laboratory in San Diego, Mr. Bloom and Mr. Maxfield, requested his help in photographing flying saucers. Flattered at the idea of assisting the U.S. military, he rigged an old plate camera to the eyepiece of his six-inch telescope and began trying to photograph the ships. Shortly afterward, as Adamski noted in *Flying Saucers Have Landed,* "I succeeded in getting what I deemed to be two good pictures of an object moving through space." He related that he turned the photographs over to Mr. Bloom and never heard from him again.

In March 1950 Adamski gave a lecture on flying saucers to the Everyman's Club in La Mesa, citing his cooperation with the military. A reporter from the *San Diego Journal* contacted the Naval Electronics Lab about the pictures and was informed that no such pictures were in their possession. Adamski was adamant about having helped Bloom and Maxfield, and a number of newspapers published stories about the dispute. Adamski assumed the status of a minor celebrity and claimed to be the victim of a government cover-up.

Now more dedicated than ever, Adamski made hundreds of photographs of objects in the sky. "During this time (1949–51) I took some five hundred photographs. But barely a dozen of them turned out good enough to preserve as proof that these craft were different from recognized Earth craft." Some of his best photographs of the spaceships were made in 1952. "The spacecraft seemed to be moving in closer to Earth, and in increasing numbers. As a result I got a number of good photographs showing well-outlined forms—but not much detail."

An article in *Fate* magazine in 1951 helped him financially by stimulating many requests for copies of his photographs, which he sold for $1.00 or $1.50. Prints bore a copyright stamp in the name of "Prof. G. Adamski" and details of when the photo was made. Adamski's audience began to grow, and soon he was getting mail from across the country requesting photographs and offering speaking engagements.

The cornerstone of Adamski's claims to extraterrestrial contact was laid on November 20, 1952, when he said he first met a long-haired Venusian in the desert near Parker, Arizona. Previously, Adamski had made several trips to the area around Desert Center, following reports of UFO landings. Two couples from Arizona—Al and Betty Bailey and "Dr." George Hunt Williamson and his wife, Betty—knew of his reputation and asked if they could accompany him on his next expedition. On this particular Thursday, Adamski, along with Lucy McGinnis (his secretary), Alice Wells, and the two Arizona couples, had just finished lunch by the roadside when they noticed a "gigantic cigar-shaped silvery ship" hovering over a nearby ridge. Sensing that the ship wanted to contact him, Adamski instructed his companions: "Someone take me down the road—quick! That ship has come looking for me and I don't want to keep them waiting!"

Lucy McGinnis and Al Bailey dropped Adamski off about a mile down the road, along with a box full of camera gear and his telescope. Soon a small silver scout ship appeared in a gully a short distance away. Adamski made a number of exposures of the ship before military planes appeared overhead and the scout ship flashed away. Suddenly, nearby, a figure beckoned to Adamski. As he approached the figure, Adamski was swept by a feeling of friendliness. "I felt like a little child in the presence of one with great wisdom and much love," Adamski wrote, "and I became very humble within myself . . . for from him was radiating a feeling of infinite understanding and kindness, with supreme humility."

The slightly built, five-foot six-inch figure in a one-piece spacesuit communicated by sign language, indicating that he was from Venus. The stranger demonstrated through signals and telepathy that his craft was powered by magnetism drawn from Earth. Adamski taught "Orthon" some English, enough so that he could say "boom, boom," expressing his concerns about Earth's atomic explosions. As the meeting drew to a close, Adamski offered one of his film holders to the Venusian, who indicated by gestures and telepathy that he would return it one day.

The other members of Adamski's group had witnessed the exchange from a distance and were naturally

★

excited when they returned to the encounter site. The only physical traces of the meeting were some footprints left by the Venusian, distinctly impressed in soft mud. Williamson made casts of the cryptic markings left by Orthon's shoes with some plaster of Paris brought along for just such a purpose, and Alice Wells made sketches.

Twenty-four days later Orthon returned to hover over Mount Palomar Gardens, and Adamski snapped the famous photographs of what came to be known as an "Adamski" saucer, with its distinctive portholes and three large condenser balls underneath the wide skirt. Before he flew away, Orthon dropped the film holder he had borrowed from Adamski, and with a wave of his hand he was gone. When developed, the plate revealed symbols similar to those left by Orthon's footprints.

The Baileys and the Williamsons took the story of the desert encounter to the *Phoenix Gazette,* which published an account illustrated with Wells's sketches on November 24, 1952. After the return of Orthon's ship Adamski offered his new photographs and story, ghost-written by Clara L. John, to British author Desmond Leslie. Leslie and his publisher, Waveney Girvan, were so impressed that they tacked Adamski's sixty pages onto a book Leslie had just written and released it as *Flying Saucers Have Landed.* Adamski became the champion of a growing community of UFO believers. The Adamski/Leslie book quickly sold over 100,000 copies, and within two years more than a dozen men and women published differing accounts of their encounters with alien beings. Adamski encouraged other contactees, accepting their stories and remaining at the center of a mutually supportive community.

It was at this time that the FBI became earnestly interested in Adamski, though not for the purpose of silencing him, as many supporters were to claim. The March 12, 1953, Riverside *Enterprise* details a talk that Adamski gave to the Lions Club of Corona, California. The article reported that Adamski had prefaced his speech with a statement that his "material has all been cleared with the Federal Bureau of Investigation and Air Force Intelligence." Several days later three FBI agents contacted Adamski at home. He denied having made the comment, and in the presence of the agents wrote a letter to this effect to the editor of the *Enterprise.* A further written statement was demanded of Adamski, indicating that he was aware of the implications of making false claims and that the FBI did not endorse individuals. A copy of this statement, witnessed by the three agents, was left with Adamski, and the FBI closed its file. During an interview several months later Adamski brandished a document bearing seals and signatures of agents, again stating that he had been "cleared" by the government agencies. Following a complaint from the Los Angeles Better Business Bureau, agents were again dispatched. A memorandum from J. Edgar Hoover's office instructed the agents to retrieve the document and to "read the riot act to him in no uncertain terms" about making false claims. Adamski was made to turn over the statement and was advised that legal action would be taken if he persisted. For years afterward he told interviewers that he had been "warned to keep quiet ... not to mention the government or any of its services" under pain of prosecution.

Throughout the 1950s Adamski was constantly in demand as a speaker and, according to his accounts, as a passenger on flying saucers. (On several occasions the space people took him on trips to the dark side of the moon in their magnetic-powered ships.) In his meetings with the space people he learned that the other planets in our solar system were arranged like grades in a school, with Earth being kindergarten. On one occasion Adamski was taken aboard a "mother" ship and introduced to a thousand-year-old master from Venus, who pointed out that sickness and old age result from not living in harmony with the universal laws under the All Supreme Intelligence. The most immediate need of the space people was to end all warfare on Earth, something they had not suffered for millions of years. The threat of nuclear devastation was a particular concern, since the radiation would severely disrupt life in the rest of the solar system. "It is a great pity that we must talk of such sorrowful things," explained Kalna, a female Venusian, "and sadder still that so much woe exists anywhere in the Universe. In ourselves, we of the other planets are not sad people. We are very gay. We laugh a great deal."

The years from 1953 to 1960 were rewarding ones for Adamski and his followers. The tensions of the Cold War fueled their conviction that they were ushering in a new dawn for Earth. "Coworker" cells sprang up in Europe, Canada, South Africa, and New Zealand. A 1959 tour of Europe

was a huge success, with Adamski meeting Queen Juliana of the Netherlands in a well-publicized event that reportedly split the royal household. The group of buildings at Mount Palomar Gardens had been expanded to accommodate the numerous people who came to partake in Adamski's "Science of Life" studies of Cosmic Law.

In 1961 Adamski turned seventy. The lectures and traveling had taxed him, and he was distraught by the sudden defection of his longtime secretary, Lucy McGinnis, on whom he had relied to give shape and expression to his thoughts. Some followers noted a slight shift in Adamski's personality, as well as a growing tendency toward spiritualism. Adamski had always maintained that his travels and communications with beings of other planets were "real," not merely mental contacts. He scoffed at reports by other contactees of psychic communications, terming them "psychic crap." Adamski also believed in the existence of the Silence Group, which attempted to discredit the study of UFOs. Psychics, he felt, often fell under the influence of this insidious group, which was controlled by world banking interests.

Adamski handed editorial control of the *Cosmic Bulletin* over to an enthusiastic coworker, Carol Honey, and declared that he would concern himself with "teaching Cosmic Philosophy." The *Bulletin* had previously contained updates on science and space research as it applied to the planets and a large question-and-answer section dealing with the space people and their plans for Earth. Now many of the *Bulletin*'s correspondents were becoming dissatisfied with the insinuation of mysticism and psychic communications into Adamski's articles. The grumbling led Honey to publish

outright accusations that Adamski himself had come under the influence of the Silence Group when it was revealed that Lucy McGinnis had left because she caught Adamski practicing trance mediumship. Shortly afterward many "coworkers" received cryptic messages from an unknown address, Box 885, Glendale. The message read, "You are doing good work. Adamski is the only one on Earth we support." Further confusion arose when Adamski was linked to newspaper advertisements that read: "Space People Need Contacts. Can you qualify? Write for free particulars. Box 885, Glendale." By the spring of 1964 the situation at Mount Palomar had deteriorated into an open palace revolt, and even Adamski's most faithful supporters were compelled to issue statements qualifying their belief in his early claims and contacts.

George Adamski arrived at Dulles Airport in February 1965, gray-skinned and drawn—not at all the healthy, tanned man with wavy silver hair that Madeleine Rodeffer and her husband had welcomed for his successful lecture tour the previous March. Unswervingly loyal, Madeleine had been busy since his last visit, showing the latest of Adamski's films to any congressman, committee, or television station she could. In January of that year a large flight of UFOs had been witnessed by government office workers on the Washington Mall, and with local interest high, Madeleine had been able to show film clips on WTOP-TV and before members of the Senate Committee on Science and Astronautics.

On the morning of February 26 an excited Adamski told Madeleine that one of the space people had stopped by on his way into town to meet with then Vice-President Humphrey. The extraterrestrial visitor told Adamski that he and Madeleine should have their movie cameras at the ready, as "they" would soon be flying by. Over breakfast, Adamski helped Madeleine load her 8mm Bell & Howell, a new camera still unfamiliar to her. Adamski kept his own 16mm camera constantly loaded. About 3 p.m., Madeleine glanced out her dining room window and glimpsed a circular object swooping in over the trees to hover in front of her house. At the same time, three men arrived at her door, announcing "They're here . . . get your cameras!" Limping, with her leg in a cast, Madeleine clomped out onto her porch but because she was unsteady handed her camera to Adamski to film the saucer. The resulting film underwent a number of mishaps in short order. Madeleine reports that when it came back from processing, several pieces were missing and several obviously faked portions had been added. The space people themselves later retrieved a portion that showed the underside of the craft in more detail than they wanted to reveal to the Earthlings.

Adamski left on a lecture tour of upper New York state and Rhode Island in mid-March. He returned to Silver Spring in early April, instructing Madeleine that his presence was to remain a secret. On April 22 he awoke with neck pains and breathing difficulties. He was sent to the Washington Sanitorium for tests and observation but refused to stay overnight.

The next morning, Adamski had a heart attack at Madeleine's home and died later that night. "The space people came to bid him farewell," Madeleine says of the February 26 encounter, "and to encourage us with our work—to getting the truth out." Working with Adamski was "the greatest feeling of helping someone who was the greatest humanitarian on Earth. I truly believe that Jesus was here on Earth."

Adamski's old friend Alice Wells said after his death that he was secretly a member of the Interplanetary Council and that in his afterlife, by special permission, he has returned to Earth. She formed the George Adamski Foundation shortly after his death, and it continues to operate out of Mount Palomar Gardens. The *Cosmic Bulletin* still provides updates on science and space research, concentrating on the Voyager interplanetary craft and their examination of other planets in our solar system. A steady number of followers still operate in many countries, notably in Europe and Japan.

"What these space people told Mr. Adamski, how they live and how they treat one another's planets," explains Madeleine, "this is what Jesus was trying to do. He was trying to open up the eyes of the people of Earth, to show we could live like that.

"*Inside the Space Ships* is next to the Bible—it's just the greatest."

Flying saucer along Highway 1.
Wabasso, Florida.
Bob Derosiers built this flying saucer in 1969,
at the time of the lunar landing. He originally
drove around town with it bolted to the roof
of his '59 Cadillac hearse, but the local
police made him remove it after they received
hundreds of calls reporting that aliens were
attacking a car. Derosiers then attached the
saucer to the dome of a grain silo and sold it to
the owner of a roadside stand that sold fruit
or antiques, depending on the season. The
business recently closed down, and Derosiers
hauled the saucer back up the road to
stand outside his woodshop in Valkaria.

Members of the New Age Foundation join hands to create a "cosmic brain battery" to summon UFOs to land at the twentieth annual New Age Convention. Mount Rainier, Washington.

On June 24, 1947, Kenneth Arnold, an Idaho businessman, was flying his light plane when he glimpsed nine gleaming disk-shaped objects whipping around the summit of Mount Rainier, Washington. He described them as looking like saucers skipping across water, and thus was born the term "flying saucers." This first well-publicized case of unexplained aerial phenomena in the United States heralded a deluge of UFO sightings and alien visitations that has yet to cease.

Every year since Arnold's sighting, UFO devotees have gathered at the foot of Mount Rainier to commemorate the event and anticipate the return of the saucers. The New Age Foundation has been holding its annual convention near the site since 1960. Wayne Aho, the founder, was affiliated with UFOs as far back as the early 1950s, when he worked on Otis T. Carr's ill-fated OTC-X1 spaceship (see page 89).

In his testimonial, *Mojave Desert Experience,* Aho writes of a visitation he experienced while attending the 1957 Interplanetary Spacecraft Convention at Giant Rock, California. He tells of sensing a strange "energy" and being drawn out alone into the desert at night. Suddenly there appeared a pulsing, glowing craft from another dimension. A telepathic voice spoke from the saucer: "Millions of souls upon the earth are awakening. I believe this civilization can be saved." Aho was directed by the extraterrestrials to buy land and create a refuge on high ground near Mount Rainier. He purchased the Cedar Park Lodge, a collection of mossy cedar-shake tourist cabins near the entrance to Mount Rainier National Park. For several days each year, before and after the anniversary of Arnold's sighting, the lodge and cabins and camp grounds are taken over by diverse saucer believers, holistic health advocates, and psychic practitioners.

The focal point of the convention is the SPLAASH site, a clearing in a druidic copse a few minutes' walk from the cabins. The Spacecraft Protective Landing Area for Advancement of Science and Humanities has, in a letter sent by Aho to state and federal authorities and the president, been declared a *"free* Landing Zone," to be maintained free of arms and open to all, alien or earthling. Several psychics and an Indian medicine chief have declared the spot to be the center of seven circles of energy. Venerable dowsers in the area report that their wands dip deeply when crossing the circle. The site functions as a year-round contact point for communication between New Agers and the Space Brothers. Members invoke the wisdom of the Brothers in deciding important questions, and a sign from the Space Brothers can be perceived in a gust of wind or a sudden parting of the clouds.

Group members converge on the SPLAASH site and, joining hands, form as large a circle as possible. Two main convergences are held each day of the convention, at early afternoon and the stroke of midnight. The more devout often maintain a vigil throughout the night, leaning against logs placed around the site and gazing into the firmament.

The ritual begins with a prayer, usually led by Harold Price, a fire-and-damnation lay preacher proclaimed Spaceport Mayor for the occasion. With eyes closed and the circle of energy completed through their clasped hands, members begin to concentrate their thoughts. Focusing their brain waves, they create a "cosmic brain battery" to summon UFOs to land. Spontaneously, one member breaks into a low incantation: "Omm, Ommmmm ..." rises slowly from the back of his throat, the consonant lengthening with each contraction of his diaphragm. One by one, people on either side pick up the mantra until the clearing is filled with deeply resonating *m*'s. Silence. Heads are slowly lifted, necks arch back until all eyes stare directly upward. No one speaks for several moments. All wait in hushed expectation for the cosmic connection or the whoosh of a saucer's drive system.

Aho or Price breaks out in song. One of the favorites, the rhythm led by an autoharp, is sung to the tune of the old camp spiritual, "Kum-Ba-Ya":

Flying saucer, Lord, kum-ba-ya
Flying saucer, Lord, kum-ba-ya
Flying saucer, Lord, kum-ba-ya
Oohhhh, Lord, kum-ba-ya

An innovation at the 1980 gathering was the inclusion of a "booster" to help harness energy. An open six-foot cube framework made from two-by-twos stood at the heart of the SPLAASH site, capped by a pyramid whose proportions duplicated those of the great pyramid of Cheops. Brushed with copper paint to increase its conductivity, the cube served as a vessel to contain the power funneled into it by the pyramid. Group members pointed out that flowers in a vase on a pedestal below the apex remained open all night and had not wilted after several days. After the invocation, several people, in a delicate mime with fingers outstretched, ran their hands over the invisible facets of the cube, by then filled with energy.

The New Age Foundation is amorphous, flexible enough in its tenets to allow believers from a broad range of other groups to attend and enjoy its functions. During the proceedings, I talked with people ranging from a successful middle-aged Seattle lawyer and his wife to Gore-Tex–clad back-to-the-landers to a group of upbeat singles in a Mercedes coupe. Participants at the convention often present lectures or lead seminars in their field of interest. Doc Johnson practices psychic chiropractic: using neural pressure points, he locates areas of weakness or ill health caused by psychic inhibitions. With his "corrections" he can multiply or reduce the power in all parts of the patient's body. Following the chiropractic workshop, he makes a pitch for a line of motor oil additives he carries as a sideline.

Jon Beckjord is well known in UFOlogy circles for his work as a Bigfoot investigator. A big blonde Swede with a Dutch-boy haircut, he walks around wearing a crumpled leather hat and L. L. Bean duckboots, indoors and out; a 16mm Bolex, held in the "present arms" position, is lashed to his left hand. He shows some films of Bigfoot, whom he holds to be a three-and-one-half dimensional creature.

Dolly, a pleasant and chubby psychic, gives demonstrations of how to sense the color and depth configurations of the human aura, while a balding fellow who lives out of his Rambler sells health pills. There are lectures and slides on Kirilian photography, displays of martial arts, people selling massage benches, health foods, Amway products, special air cleaners for automobiles, and, of course, books.

Late into the night, Aho himself gives a talk to the general assembly, sitting cross-legged in the tiered bunks around the walls of the ski house. New Agers believe that Earth is undergoing a major cyclical change, for which mankind is at present profoundly unprepared. A letter to the president of the United States urges that a summit conference of "aware individuals" be called to help "identify and make recommendations for NEW DIRECTION." The projected disasters include the eruption of Mount St. Helens (which did happen) and the collapse of the West Coast into the sea along the San Andreas Fault and subsequent tidal wave inundating Japan and Washington State up to Mount Rainier (which hasn't happened yet). Fossil fuels and internal combustion engines represent wrong thinking. Holistic healing and the use of free energy by flying saucers represent right thinking.

"All the psychiatrists and counselors in the world cannot solve all the anxiety problems. Could it be that man is being *forced* into new directions?" asks Aho. "With the threatened oil economy and inflation, perhaps the plug holding back human progress can be withdrawn. Because of a number of wrong choices, mankind is now faced with the threat of bare survival as the planet enters a recurring change ... a 'major cycle' as described by UFO occupants."

The first time I met Wayne Aho, I had driven up the coast from California in late November and arrived at his door on a dark and snowy night. He invited me in: "Come in and be at peace. Know that you've been examined before you came and you must be okay or you would not have been allowed to come. The Space Brothers are watching out for us, seeing that none of us comes to harm and that only the right people come here."

I left early the next morning with a copy of *Mojave Desert Experience* which Aho had given me. It was inscribed, "Best wishes for the New Age."

This display at the 1981 New Age Convention was set up by Dr. Edward M. Palmer, who runs the Cosmic Science Research Center in Portland, Oregon. The center, which maintains a meeting room and a newsletter, dedicates itself to "publishing and teaching the expanded teachings of Jesus and other world teachers and servants, and the Hierarchical Intelligences and Beings on the various planes of consciousness."

Palmer used to travel around the country with Wayne Aho during the late 1950s and early '60s, renting community halls for twenty-five dollars a night to lecture about UFOs and their message for Earth. They were a Mutt and Jeff team, going from town to town in their old Ford, posting handbills and believing themselves to be in the vanguard of a new truth. Now that Aho's New Age Foundation is drawing media attention from the "Real People" television show, he tends to ignore his old fellow missionary, and Palmer is bitter in remembering the time he gave Aho his last five dollars to get to the next town.

Dr. Palmer currently serves as the medium for an interplanetary being named Ashtar Rayonda, who says that cosmic plans for restoring the planet to its original beauty will be greatly facilitated "if you will maintain a feeling of friendly interest and confidence in us and in mind hold a thought of welcome."

A stand at the New Age Convention.
Mount Rainier, Washington.

Harold Pym with his painting
The Earth is the LORD'S, at the New
Age Convention. Mount Rainier,
Washington.

Carl Gendreau predicts that an airliner
and a UFO will meet within three years.
San Bernardino, California.

had heard there was a saucer at the Olive Dell Nudist Ranch somewhere south of San Bernardino. After driving several days, I still couldn't find it. One has to ask a nudist where a nudist ranch is, and I didn't know any. At the end of a hot day, I came across a potholed asphalt road, evidently abandoned, the way barred by a rusting wire gate. Signs on the gate read *Stop, World Art,* and *Keep Out.* The lure of *World Art* overshadowed the stricture of *Stop* and *Keep Out.* I trespassed.

The road wound through hills covered with sage and greasewood. After several miles, a little red-haired man wearing a toque popped his head out around a knoll. He saw my car, ducked down, and ran away like a gnome. I pulled off the road, dipping through mesquite, rocks, and rubble to chase him. Suddenly he pulled up short and motioned for me to follow. His camp consisted of a tent and a '62 Meteor parked in a gully, on lands that had once been an agricultural research station. We found Carl Gendreau painting there. His back was toward us and as he heard our footsteps on the gravel he turned, whipped out the painting from behind him, and said, "How do you like this one?"

The painting depicts an encounter between a commercial airliner and a mother spaceship. Carl predicted that this meeting would occur within three years. On and around the car lay some of his other paintings. Most were surrealistic: people walking along an off-this-world checkerboard

or winged white horses flying through yards of yellow silk billowing in a mauve-tinted sky. His easel was the rear window of the Meteor, and he used its hubcaps for palettes. A kind, soft-spoken man, Carl proved easy to photograph. He really didn't care how the world saw him. He and Arthur, the red-haired gnome, had arrived a few weeks earlier on the doorstep of World Art, a company set up to make reproductions of famous paintings. Carl and Arthur had come from Mount Shasta, traditionally considered holy by the Klamath Indians and, more recently, by the I AM sect.

I AM had been established back in 1934 by Guy Ballard and his wife, Edna. Ballard announced that he had been visited by the Comte de St. Germain while on "government business" in the Grand Teton Mountains. St. Germain told Ballard that he and his wife had been selected by a group of "Ascended Masters" to lead America and the rest of the world into a new Golden Age. (The Ascended Masters were superhuman semideities who had broken out of the reincarnation cycle and now wielded fabulous powers.) Guy and Edna, now "The Accredited Messengers of St. Germain," soon took over a major part of William Pelley's fascist "Silver Shirt" movement and coopted some of its ideology. During the Depression thousands crowded into the I AM churches to partake in the patriotic "New Thought" crusade. Large audiences shouted orders in unison to the Cosmic Forces to "blast and annihilate" the evils created by the Black Magicians: the Dope Beast, Labor Agitation, Alcohol, and Communism.

Since the 1940s I AM has been more temperate, with a much smaller though stable following. Each year at its Mount Shasta headquarters the church holds an extravagant pageant culminating with the reenactment of Christ's ascension into the ranks of the Ascended Masters.

Though not members of I AM, both Carl and Arthur followed its teachings. They told me about spiritual healings and recommended special teas and herbs. Atomic testing and the potential for global destruction were upsetting the balance of the universe, they said, and a convoy of ships from various planets constantly monitors the situation. The saucers of the Space Brothers and the Ascended Masters will arrive first at Mount Shasta, bringing health and healing for mankind.

Moving from town to town, Carl and Arthur supported themselves by selling paintings from vacant lots. The police persecuted them, they said, because they knew the truth about the government and the way things were being run. They were always forced to move on, driving their battered white Meteor with the psychedelic hubcaps.

I went back in 1978. World Art was closed up. A young man living there told me that Carl Gendreau and his red-haired friend had stopped by once. There has not been a trace of either of them since.

★

Evan Hayworth and the Interstellar
Technical Research Billenium Falcon.
Venice, California. See page 60.

Constant Bilodeau at his Centre de
Conscience Cosmique—Cénacle de
Notre Dame de L'Espace (Center of
Cosmic Consciousness—Cenacle of
Our Lady of Outer Space). St. Jovite,
Quebec. See page 60.

As chief designer and promoter for Interstellar Technical Research of Venice, California, Evan Hayworth designs everything from information-retrieval systems to playground equipment. The primary mission of the Billenium Falcon is hauling I.T.R.'s model solar system around to elementary schools to interest six-graders in outer space and astronomy. Patterned after Hans Solo's Millennial Falcon from the film *Star Wars*, the 1960 station wagon has been customized by design and by accidents such as the "alien sneak attack" that crumpled the Falcon's hood and grille.

Constant Bilodeau runs his Centre de Conscience Cosmique from a converted wood-frame church several miles outside the town of St. Jovite, seventy-five miles north of Montreal. The center has been in existence since 1975, when Bilodeau first received a "metaphysique"—a message about the future of the world. The voice of the message told Bilodeau that the future of the world depended on man's embracing his true spiritual nature and seeking communion with a higher "order of being."

In his search for greater understanding of his own metaphysical experiences Bilodeau encountered the book *OAHSPE*, first published in 1882 by a New Yorker, John Ballou Newbrough. *OAHSPE* is "a sacred history of the dominions of the higher and lower heavens of the Earth for the last 79,000 years," related to Newbrough by Jehovih's "Angelic Ambassadors" using automatic writing. Within its three-quarters of a million words and 1,008 pages *OAHSPE* presents "authentic and official disclosures made for our orientation and guidance by organized space-dwelling entities above us in the hierarchy of life forms.

The present era in Newbrough's tome is referred to as the "Kosmon Age," a time when Jehovih's plan for earthly perfection nears fulfillment in the new-birthright land of America. The *OAHSPE* cosmology portrays ascending Earthlings as "I'hins," the half-breed offspring of angels and primitive man. The I'hins are caught in mortal battle with the dark lower forces of mankind, the "Druks." Many modern ideas and phenomena appear in *OAHSPE*, among them the Van Allen belt in outer space, radiation and nuclear war, and "fire-boats"—large interstellar islands of flaring light used to transport angels around the galaxies. Many events of recent history, particularly American history, are portrayed as divine conflicts necessary to establish dominion over America. The angels on their fire-boats oversee and protect the leaders of the new spiritual land while themselves battling negative forces in the heavens.

OAHSPE remained an obscure text for many years until it surfaced as a mainstay of *Search* magazine in the mid-1950s. *Search* presented its readers with a wide range of information about such paranormal phenomena as UFOs, pyramid power, alien cultures, reincarnation, and self-help programs for the metaphysically inclined. It was through *Search* that Bilodeau came to study *OAHSPE*. The teachings confirmed for him not only his own metaphysical experience but also his previous sighting of a large glowing light in the sky. "The flying saucer represents both the physical and the metaphysical," he said. "It occurs on all the aspects, all the planes."

★

essie Van Boren lives in Fort Sumner, the burial place of the outlaw Billy the Kid. A widow, she owns the Pecos Oil Company, which she and her husband began in the Depression, pumping gas by hand out of forty-five-gallon drums for Oklahoma farmers doing their best to get out of the dust bowl. Her efforts paid off, and she now lives comfortably, able to pursue her ambitions as an artist. Her business card introduces her as "Bessie Van Boren, Painter of Western and Modern Art."

In her front yard behind a gateway of welded horseshoes stands a large steel silhouette of an athletic human form with one arm upraised. Reminiscent of the Vic Tanny's Health Spa man, the "Man of Progress" holds not an Olympian torch but an army surplus bomb, which he metaphorically launches into the future, while reaching back for another. Among the art works that Bessie is most proud of is her painting *The Crucifixion of Peace,* which illustrates her belief that society and the church are in a state of collapse. The global future does not look good, and in Bessie's estimation the only people saved will be those who, as in the painting, can get in a rocket and escape Earth. "Humanity's only chance," she believes, "is in outer space."

Bessie Van Boren with her painting
The Crucifixion of Peace. Fort Sumner,
New Mexico.

Members of the Aetherius Society
charge a Spiritual Battery. Hollywood,
California.

In 1954 George King, a thirty-five-year-old bachelor, was washing dishes in his London flat when he received a disembodied command, "Prepare yourself, you are to become the voice of the Interplanetary Parliament." Several days later, while King was in a meditative trance, an Indian yoga master entered his apartment and informed him that the Cosmic Intelligences, who were manning spacecraft above Earth, had selected him to act as the Primary Terrestrial Channel for important messages they were about to begin transmitting to Earth. Immersing himself in yogic-Samadhic trances, King soon established telepathic contact with a Cosmic Master on Venus, named Aetherius. This highly evolved being revealed to King the spiritual hierarchy of the universe. The Cosmic Masters (including Jesus Christ, Mars Sector 6, and Jupiter 92) met as the Interplanetary Parliament on Saturn. Here on Earth, Aetherius explained, a secret spiritual order of reincarnated perfected beings formed the Great White Brotherhood.

In January 1955 King gave the first public demonstration of his contacts with the Cosmic Master in London's Caxton Hall, a meeting center for occult groups. He mounted the platform, entered a trance, and Aetherius, using King's voice, revealed the "Cosmic Plan for the Peace and Enlightenment of the People of Earth." Initially, King attracted only a few followers. The Aetherius history notes: "In the early days he had to face much prejudice and opposition from all sides. He stood alone, save for one or two people who recognized that the contact was in every way genuine." King's lectures grew longer, more frequent, and more urgent. Other Masters and members of the Great White Brotherhood began communicating with King during his trances. Speaking engagements at other metaphysical groups, followed by dramatic trance sessions on radio and television, began to enhance his reputation.

King founded the Aetherius Society in August 1956, charged by Aetherius with the task of helping bring Devic stability to Earth by promoting metaphysical knowledge about the Cosmic Masters and their healing practices and by exposing the dangers to the solar system threatened by atomic bomb testing. The messages and news that King received, along with accounts of flying-saucer sightings, were featured in the group's magazine, *Cosmic Voice*. These transmissions were reprinted as books, as was Jesus' Aquarian-Age Bible to Earth—*The Twelve Blessings*. Jesus was revealed to King during a group ritual on top of Holdstone Down, Devon, in July 1958. From that time forward, King was commissioned to "act as an essential link between Earth and the Higher Forces" in the "charging" of eighteen Holy Mountains throughout the world. The Cosmic Energy stored in these mountains could later be released through prayer to alleviate the suffering of mankind. "Operation Starlight," as the task of climbing and charging the mountains was known, is described in Aetherius literature as "the greatest single Metaphysical Task ever undertaken upon Earth since Her inception as a Planet."

As part of the world mission of Operation Starlight, King set sail for America in 1959, taking along one disciple. Invitations to talk had been obtained from flying-saucer, metaphysical, and Theosophical groups across the country, and whenever possible King was also to make radio or television appearances. He won an enthusiastic audience at the first national convention of the Amalgamated Flying Saucer Clubs of America, in Los Angeles. Conservatively dressed, he appeared on stage with his assistant, who quieted the audience and forbade anyone to enter or leave the auditorium or to take flash pictures. King, with his head bowed, donned a pair of dark goggles. After several minutes of silence, his head jerked up and he began his speech: "This is Mars sector 6 speaking." The enthusiasm of the audience was intensified by the revelation that only members of the Aetherius Society would be told when the end of civilization was near, so they could go to the top of the charged mountains and thus be saved. Encouraged by the American response, King moved to Los Angeles in 1960 and incorporated there as a nonprofit religious organization. He had advanced from "unworthy and ignorant servant" to colleague, confidant, and even advisor to those who had been his superiors. Jesus, in a 1959 transmission, told him, "My Son, you are now one of Us, and We now declare this to all men."

King no longer gives public transmissions of the Masters' messages; instead, he concentrates the efforts of the society and its members on harnessing and directing healing psychic energies throughout the world, under the guidance of the Masters. The society views itself as a service organization, providing "the thin White line" of defense against the karmic evil and greed of men, and they put great emphasis on quantifiable results. Reports following Phase 8 of their Saturn Mission hail "another spiritual triumph" "responsible for saving 720,000 people from death or severe mutilation from natural catastrophe." "This is not," concludes a report in the *Cosmic Voice,* "some vague discussion by so-called 'Spiritual workers' sitting around the feet of a flower-carrying Yogi, wondering how to help their ignorant brothers on Earth."

My first meeting with the Aetherius Society was interrupted by a great slamming of doors and the sound of wet boots slogging down the hall. The door of the room where I was being interviewed by Dr. Alan Moseley opened to reveal a man wearing a dripping army poncho and an Australian bush hat with water sluicing off the brim. His accent, like Moseley's, was solidly British. This visitor informed us that His Eminence, Prince George King de Santorini,

Display at Aetherius headquarters depicting the position of the governing spaceship, Saturn 6, over the logos of Mother Earth. Hollywood, California.

Display of radionics equipment built
by Aetherians for Operation
Bluewater. Hollywood, California.

Count de Florina, was due to arrive shortly from the successful completion of Phase 4 of the Saturn Mission at Lake Powell, Utah. I was instructed to return the following evening, at which time (barring catastrophic events somewhere in the world) I would receive the mantra training that would allow me to participate in Operation Prayer Power. Like Operations Starlight, Bluewater, Karmalight, and Sunbeam, Operation Prayer Power is one of the Aetherius Society's "Divine Missions" to enlighten and save mankind.

The following evening, while waiting for my training, I wandered around the unrestricted areas of the American headquarters. (The group has branches in Canada, Europe, England, New Zealand, Ghana, and Nigeria.) The Aetherius Society occupies a compound of stucco buildings in a style known as "Hollywood Moorish," just a few blocks from the excesses of Sunset and Vine in Hollywood. The front door of the main building opens into a wide hallway that also serves as a bookstore and an exhibition hall of Aetherius projects and the "radionics" equipment used in its operations. Stones from each of the eighteen Holy Mountains (among them Mount Baldy and Mount Kilimanjaro), mounted in gold pendants or on polished wooden bases, are sold to those members unable to make their own pilgrimages to the peaks. The power of these stones had been rendered more potent through the blessings bestowed on them by King. Books printed in the Aetherius printshop include *The Great White Brotherhood Accept Initiates* (future prospects for devoted Aetherians); *You Are Responsible!* (the vital role of Aetherians in deflecting an attack by evil life forms from outside the universe), and *The Day the Gods Came* (spacecraft manipulate cosmic energies to facilitate the arrival of Earth's Cosmic Master).

At the far end of the hallway, framed by a proscenium and velvet curtains, is an elaborate display about Operation Bluewater. A large plexiglass pyramid, enclosing copper coils and wires connected to smaller rectangular blue boxes, dominates the display. Photographs show this same pyramid full of radionics equipment, which had been designed by King and built by Aetherians in their shop, being submerged behind a power boat with King at the helm. Guided by the Masters, King had towed the "energy radiator" through intricate maneuvers over a "Psychic Centre" located in the ocean off Santa Catalina Island. The energy from the Cosmic Intelligences was thus transmitted to the "complex, subtle nerve membranes leading from the Psychic Centre, to other parts of the great body of the breathing Mother Earth." The success of this operation is demonstrated to Aetherians by the fact that the West Coast has not suffered the long-predicted earthquake that would have sent it into the sea.

My training for the prayer session, conducted under the watchful eyes of two middle-aged female Aetherians, takes only a few minutes. Feet together, palms facing forward, elbows tucked tight to my sides, I push the mantra, "Om mani padme hum," out from my diaphragm to the satisfaction of my tutors. Members arrive several minutes early for the regular Thursday night prayer session so that the directors can regulate the group's breathing. Aetherius protocol requires members to have showered recently and to have abstained from alcohol before the Prayer Power sessions. A dress code of tie and jacket for men and dresses for women is observed.

The Spiritual Battery, covered with a cloth and mounted on a surveyor's tripod, is the focal point of the room. A choir-robed member sits at a folding camp table to one side. With stopwatch in hand, the timekeeper transcribes into a ledger the precise number of participants and the minutes of prayer energy focused into the battery. Batlike in his robes, with white-gloved hands stretched above his head, Dr. Charles Abrahamson, a senior member of the society, holds a silent countdown to the stroke of 7:30. At that exact moment Abrahamson sweeps his arms downward and the group of forty-five charges into the Holy Mantra, "Om mani padme hum . . . OM mani padme Hum . . . *OM* mani padme HUM." Abrahamson exhorts the group into a rapid, emphatic

chant. "Deeper, deeper!" he commands. The response, though spirited, never reaches a level of euphoric rapture. Rather, like most of Aetherius's workings, it remains efficient, almost military in its precision.

Once the group is rolling well with the mantra, the specially trained Prayer Team advances in single file toward the battery. The lead team member proceeds alone to within a few feet of the battery and recites the first of the Twelve Blessings. The first cycle of the Prayer Power session lasts twenty-five minutes, followed by a five-minute break for a stroll on the front lawn and a glass of water. A ten-minute break is called after the next cycle of forty-five minutes. The Prayer Team continues to recite the Twelve Blessings in turn throughout the second and third cycles of the evening.

Following the third cycle I was given a few minutes to take my photographs. The Spiritual Battery, nearing its full-charge capacity of 700 prayer-hours, was carefully capped and taken to safe storage. As the battery and its escort made their way through the crowded room, the members cautiously fell back from it. It was felt that with so much power stored in the battery, an inadvertent mishap could have devastating results for life, limb, and karma. King maintains that the specialized radionics

★

equipment he has developed is capable of storing this spiritual energy for up to 10,000 years, to be released as needed. Several batteries are kept permanently charged, ready to forestall world crises. Numerous examples of the past efficacy of Aetherius projects can be cited by members.

Great demands are placed on the few to balance mankind's karmic deficit. Many members devote more than forty hours a week to Aetherius in addition to holding regular jobs. "We have no deadwood," notes Edna Spencer, a twenty-five-year veteran of the society. Services are held Sunday and Monday evenings, with classes and lectures offered throughout the week, in addition to the Thursday night Prayer Power sessions. A Doctor of Metapsychics degree—signifying "a hierarchy of sanctification which the 'unilluminated' are excluded from attaining"—is awarded to senior members of King's College of Spiritual Sciences.

King's own tireless dedication to the Cosmic Plan stands in stark contrast to his ill health. For some time he lived quietly at the Hollywood compound until, at the urging of the Masters, a more restful retreat was purchased in Santa Barbara. Concern for the future of Aetherius, not just mankind, now preoccupies King. Recognizing that he must, in time, "vacate the physical planes of Earth," he has begun preparing for the continuation of Aetherius. King's position within the history of the universe has been assured: his name is enshrined in the Official Records of the Great White Brotherhood and the master tapes of his transmissions are stored in perpetuity in "the strongest vault in England."

A senior member, recalling King's preparations for a solo mission over one of Earth's Psychic Centres, writes: "... we could not help but think of our Leader and Spiritual Master at this crucial moment. What thoughts must have been passing through his mind?

"What anxieties—yes, human feelings of anxiety and concern—must have been invading his consciousness at such a moment? How alone he must have felt ... we gazed in wonder and awe at this single individual, who has won for the Forces of Light ... great shining victories over and over again.

"If ever a man deserved to be followed, then he surely must be the one!"

Project Starlight International,
a research complex of lights, radio,
and laser gear for signaling UFOs,
constructed by the Association for the
Understanding of Man (AUM).
Near Austin, Texas.

Project Starlight International was introduced to the public in 1975 by a glossy brochure featuring photographs of an outdoor site where serious young men wearing horn-rimmed glasses and white coveralls monitored switches or spoke into microphones surrounded by banks of electronic gadgetry: video screens with cryptic lists of numbers, VHS decks, and graph-paper recorders. The facility, secreted northwest of Austin, Texas, was announced by its founder and director, Ray Stanford, to be the world's first and only full-time site for "hard-data" monitoring and recording of unidentified aerial phenomena.

Project Starlight International's working procedures were outlined at the 1976 MUFON (Mutual UFO Network) symposium in Ann Arbor, Michigan. Stanford's polished presentation and photographs were met with enthusiasm and whispered amazement at the sophistication and cost of the endeavor. Many felt that the time was finally at hand when the study coming to be known as "UFOlogy" would be freed from the stigma of irrational amateurism.

I first heard about PSI in the fall of 1977, while I was in California visiting Orlando Toroni, who had his own scaled-down version of PSI's light-decoy concept (see pages 76–77). Toroni showed me the slick PSI brochure and commented ruefully on the scornful response his work had gotten from Stanford. I attempted to arrange a visit to Stanford's lab site, but without success. Visits were out

of the question, Stanford told me over the phone. The staff was in the midst of some very critical analysis, and important public announcements would be made in the months to come. But by 1978 people were scratching their heads trying to remember when they had last heard about Stanford and the "cutting-edge" investigations of PSI. The sudden brilliance of Ray Stanford and Project Starlight International had flared and vanished like a meteor over the central Texas skies.

It took until April 1982 for me to arrange an interview with Stanford. What was to be a short run-through of the PSI foray into UFO research ended by encompassing Stanford's entire career, from his early initiation as a contactee to his current theory of flying-saucer propulsion, "Magneto Hydrodynamic Drive Systems." It soon became apparent that the complex history of Project Starlight International and the motivations behind it could only be understood by examining the mercurial personality of Ray Stanford.

The Stanford brothers, Ray and Rex, grew up in Corpus Christi, Texas. While still quite young, they produced several books that recounted their own experiences as UFO contactees. (One of these was coauthored by John McCoy, who had also helped the famed 1950s contactee George Hunt Williamson with the widely read *UFOs Confidential* and operated the Essene Press in Corpus Christi.) Ray had his first "very distinct telepathic message from the space people" in December 1954, when he was only sixteen years old. His first personal contact with a flying saucer occurred

a year later, at night on a hillside outside Brownsville, Texas. Ray, Rex, and a friend were held in a state of paralysis, unable to speak, while a saucer with pulsing lights and a throbbing hum held them in its glare.

In 1957 Ray and Rex hitchhiked to California to meet the most famous of all contactees, George Adamski (see pages 43-48). For the young Ray Stanford, the happenings at Adamski's Mount Palomar retreat were exotic enough in themselves to serve as an out-of-this-world experience. Adamski quickly took a liking to the naïve Texan, who describes himself at that time as "fast-talking and excitable." Adamski's Palomar Gardens was a remote haven of easy living just down the slope from the Mount Palomar Observatory. Members of the Beat generation would often make the weekend trek down from Los Angeles to meet "the Prof." Long into the night, accompanied by song and guitar, Adamski would chronicle his UFO joyrides and relay messages from Orthon, his Venusian contact. Hangers-on included a shifting coterie of rich older women, seemingly attracted to the aging though still rugged and virile Adamski. Another regular was Sonja, who had developed a prodigious reputation for her alleged "close encounters of the fourth kind" with a number of spacemen.

Stanford, confident that he was among the blessed who had made contact with the alien world, quickly learned the repertoire of then-current UFO lore and Adamski's teachings. Toward the end of the brothers' stay at Mount Palomar, Adamski, often in

★

his cups from too much eggnog, revealed candid glimpses of his past.

"Hell, you boys don't know what a damn man that Roosevelt was!" the Polish-born Adamski said to Ray one evening. "He was the worst damn president we ever had! DAMN! That Prohibition was a good thing for me, boys. You're too young to know about it, but hell, they outlawed the liquor all over the country. Hell, I got the Royal Order of Tibet—all incorporated and everything! I got the special license—for religious purposes I can make the wine. Gottdammit! Hell, I made enough wine for all of Southern California! I was making a fortune. Then that man Roosevelt, he knock out the Prohibition. Hell, if it hadn't been for that gottdamned man Roosevelt—I wouldn't had to get into this saucer crap."

"He didn't want us to grow old," suggests Stanford, "waiting around for Orthon."

Ray and Rex, dressed in identical suits, went out on the road, preaching the news of psychic communication and alien contact in rented halls from Bakersfield, California, to Holbrook, Arizona. An impassioned orator, Ray began conducting spiritualist readings and psychic healings in northern Arizona in 1961. The group that began to form around him was a cross section of what sociologists call "the cultic milieu," and included businessmen, a physicist, several high school students, electronic engineers, and the owner of a health food store, who injected most of the needed funds.

Along with Stanford's growing awareness of his abilities as a psychic came his interest in an instrumented approach to UFOs. It was at this time that he coined the name Association for the Understanding of Man (AUM) for his study group and Project Starlight International (PSI) for his developing concept for interacting with UFOs. In 1964 members of AUM constructed a ring of lights out in the desert to signal UFOs by transmitting in Morse code the mathematical equation for "Inverse Pi." The experiment failed to attract a saucer to land or to get one to repeat the sequence of flashing lights. Nonetheless, Stanford intimates that the project was responsible for a rash of sightings in the area.

In the mid-1960s Rex swore off UFOs and returned to college to become a parapsychologist. Ray left the Arizona group in 1967 over an undisclosed dispute and settled in San Antonio, intent on pursuing his interest in painting and a degree in art history. His reputation as a psychic had preceded him, and many of his weekends were spent commuting to Austin from San Antonio, catering to the demands of a number of spiritual healing groups in that city. At the urging of several people he had helped, Stanford gave up his art studies and moved to Austin in 1969.

The second Association for the Understanding of Man was incorporated in March 1971, as an openmembership, nonprofit corporation. Its stated goals were the "studies of the physical, mental and spiritual natures of man" and "attunement with *Reality* or *Being Itself*." Stanford made five psychic readings the next year, dealing both with traditional spiritual themes and with the threat of a nuclear apocalypse that would destroy the Earth. Sections of the readings suggest that members might have a hand in averting such a catastrophe: "Events could modify the sequence and the development of that [nuclear war] slightly, but love and mercy and repentance on the part of many—or *even a few sufficiently diligent*—could transform it into a pattern of grace where it need not come to pass."

The period from 1971 to '76 was the halcyon time for AUM. A periodic newsletter and quarterly journal kept members across the United States in touch with the latest developments in consciousness. A reliable staff of young, educated volunteers helped run the Austin office, edit the newsletters, and pay the bills. A loyal core of AUM members supported Stanford and his readings, believing that he was the instrument on Earth of the all-seeing, all-knowing cosmic guardians known as the White Brotherhood.

The resources and finances of AUM members were first pressed into PSI projects in 1972, but it wasn't until 1975, when several AUM members moved to Austin and devoted themselves to PSI fieldwork, that the project really began to roll. Money flowed in and immediately ways arose to spend it. A list soliciting funds for equipment cited twenty items, including an automatic recording magnetometer, recording gravimeters, ambient thermometers, a large parabolic microphone, an eight-channel chart

★

recorder, and a bank of radio frequency scanners and radar. Many of these pieces were eventually purchased.

A seminal piece of equipment was a Stanford-designed device called a UFO/VECTOR. Part telescope, part video camera and ruby laser, the UFO/VECTOR was "to evaluate whether or not UFO intelligences are capable of, or interested in, exchanging intelligent communication." Electronic connections were provided to translate messages to the UFO via laser light pulses. A prerecorded message of welcome to the presumably friendly aliens was kept on hand for transmission. The apparatus was to be aimed at the UFO by the operator watching a television screen and moving a "joy stick" to align the UFO image with an aiming mark on the TV screen. "An optical aiming mode" was also available, as well as protective goggles for the operator in case the UFO responded with a dangerous blast of light.

Stanford asserted that the UFO/VECTOR could be used to test the hypothesis that UFOs caused atmospheric density variations round themselves, which would sharply bend light beams. This aspect was dismissed by a PSI volunteer: "Stanford insisted on saying it every chance he got because he didn't want people to think he had the laser just to *talk* to UFOs. Some people thought that trying to *communicate* with UFOs was kind of kooky."

The cost of the elaborate components for the research facility was high, and it often led to divisive arguments among those members with a

degree of technical knowledge and Stanford. As one former member noted, " 'true believers' always felt that everything would turn out well in the not-so-long run, since Stanford was the tool of these exalted '[Space] Brothers'.... They felt strongly that Stanford's *inspirations* regarding equipment needed, etc., should not be gainsaid, especially since the 'Brothers' usually specifically endorsed expensive or controversial ideas."

Progress reports from the PSI lab stopped abruptly in the fall of 1977. The UFO community at large, however, believed that the work was still being carried out, that the magnetometer waited on standby, that a steady stream of volunteers watched the night skies north of Lake Travis. In fact, very few night watches were maintained after September 1977, and only one in 1978.

Stanford had what one AUM member termed "a religious experience" in 1977 and stopped all psychic readings. Disillusioned by the realization that most of the AUM members had not been moved to search for spirituality in themselves, Stanford refused all requests to resume his readings. "I think the person most harmed by the psychic readings was me," Stanford said in a recent interview. "There's no hope—you can't get through to these people—they always want to be following some hero and be duped. And I said, 'That's the end of it, I'm going to become an artist, I'll pursue the UFO thing as I can ... and not contribute to spiritual delinquency anymore.' "

Most of the AUM office staff left in 1978, and most of the PSI volunteers left shortly afterward when they failed to get Stanford to continue his

psychic readings. Stanford retreated to his office, analyzing, with an assistant, a Super 8 film of a UFO photographed through the window of an airliner. Money for PSI still trickled in, though not at the previous rate. Bob Dunnam, a supporter and AUM member for many years, maintained his faith in Stanford's work. "The UFO work continued after that, PSI continued for a couple, three years. I helped support Ray for a while during that time. Really it kind of broke up when I stopped supporting it. The primary reason is simply that Ray had developed what I thought was pretty good material—some pretty good insights. I think that to this day. But Ray never got around to really codifying and writing it up, and doing various things that would support his theories. He never got the material ... he never really wrote it down and I got tired of waiting for that to happen.... I'd still like to see him write the book. I think he's got some pretty good data."

Lake City UFO Landing Port. Lake City,
Pennsylvania.

The Lake City UFO Landing Port was built in 1976 by citizens of that town as their community bicentennial project. City administrators and advertising pamphlets for the site declare it to be the "1st UFO Landing Port in the World," although that distinction properly belongs to the town of St. Paul, Alberta. The park is equipped with radio homing beacons to attract cruising flying saucers and lights to illuminate the raised earthen pad. On special days a team of two little green alien figures are placed around the fiberglass saucer. At the municipal campground next door, postcards, commemorative license plates, and bumper stickers bearing the design of a pulsing UFO are sold.

Donald Tome, who maintains the park, is the former police chief of Lake City. He left the frustrations of that job for one that "brings happiness to myself and others."

Donald Tome at the Lake City UFO Landing Port. Lake City, Pennsylvania.

Orlando Toroni spends his nights on a hillside tracking spaceships hiding behind satellites. Near Orland, California.

★

We're heading up into the hills above Orland, California, in Orlando's old Buick, and the tie rod ends are shot. Every bump throws the car into a fit of shaking, and Orlando has to back off the gas and bull the car back onto the curve of the road, winding up and up above the valley floor. The sun is setting, sinking the landscape into a dull rose glow as we climb above the almond groves, past the olive trees, to where the heat and dust haze clear away.

We reach a step on the side of Red Mountain, just below the summit, several thousand feet above a valley running eastward to the Sacramento River. Orlando stops the car and begins unpacking his equipment. An armored case holds the two aircraft traffic lights that are the backbone of his operation. Snapped inside the lid of the case, with shadow drawings to show where each belongs, are a first-aid kit, flares, a compass, and a flashlight. Stowed in the trunk are warm clothes, an army cot, and blankets for the colder nights, when viewing is best.

Orlando connects one of the traffic lights to his car battery and begins his vigil, scanning the skies through binoculars. The long steady arc of a satellite in orbit is readily visible to the naked eye. Believing that the extraterrestrials conceal themselves behind satellites, he starts to signal with his lamp, using random blips, Morse code, and light filters for various combinations of colors.

Orlando's curiosity about UFOs was first piqued in 1969, the year of the lunar landing, by the headlines emblazoned on magazines and tabloids at the supermarket check-out counter. He began to pick up books on the subject and in 1972 made his first trip to Red Mountain, where he spent a few hours peering into the night sky. By the end of that year, he recalls feeling obsessed, awakening from sleep, drawn to the hillside. Finding the aircraft traffic lights in an army surplus store galvanized Toroni into action, and the project began to solidify into an efficient routine. The growing disintegration of American life and ideals during the late 1960s and early '70s fueled his ambition. "I would stand up there for hours looking for answers in the sky and begin to cry," he recently recalled. "I felt I'd been ordained to help."

Extraterrestrials cruising the night sky sometimes engaged him in a cosmic "Wink, wink, I see you blink" game, in response to his encoded messages. Attempts to communicate with other groups involved in "scientific" efforts to contact extraterrestrials proved disappointing. Ray Stanford, of Project Starlight International (see pages 71–73), considered Toroni's equipment crude and his methods inadequate; Orlando believes that Stanford was miffed by his own lack of success with lasers, video, and other expensive paraphernalia.

Orlando was an unemployed "cat-skinner" (bulldozer operator) when I met him in 1977. At his small bungalow he talked about the extraterrestrials and their relationship to Earth. Omniscient and omnipotent agents of divine retribution, they watched from their vantage points behind the satellites. They were concerned, as Orlando was himself, with the fate of post-Watergate America—an America he saw being destroyed by corruption. Sitting with his wife, Hannah, on the sofa, he showed me passages in the family Bible, underlined with a yellow marker, that he believed described the appearances of flying saucers.

In 1980 I tried to locate Orlando and his family but was unsuccessful until I recently found him in Eureka, California, living with a group of born-again Christians. He had grown increasingly troubled, he says, throughout 1978 and '79, out of work and out of luck. He took to drinking and living mean until Hannah took the kids and left in '80. After his second attempt at suicide, he heard the call of the Lord. "He turned my life around. . . . I've been a seeker all my life, serious and alone . . . but none of it bothers me now—I've come to a peace and joy I'd never thought possible."

What did he think about UFOs at this point, I asked him. "I feel they are part of Satan's work, part of his deceptions. That doesn't mean that they are not perhaps *real* in the way that we know it, but they are not of Christ."

George Van Tassel constructed the
Integratron, a device for retarding the
aging process, from plans received
from a space being named Solganda.
Giant Rock, California.

"A modern John the Baptist, crying in the wilderness, 'Prepare ye for a new cosmic age!'" writes an early chronicler of the UFO scene describing George Van Tassel.

Throughout the frenetic 1950s Van Tassel was considered by many believers to be the prophet of the flying-saucer movement. His wilderness was a tract of land in the Mojave Desert, north of Twenty-Nine Palms, a wind-ravaged sweep of sand dominated by a solitary, sixty-foot-high granite boulder called Giant Rock. Van Tassel was responsible for two widely publicized things of enduring importance to saucer believers: the Integratron, a device constructed under the tutelage of space beings to retard the aging process of Earthlings, and the annual Interplanetary Spacecraft Convention, held from 1954 until 1977.

An airline mechanic and flight-test engineer, Van Tassel fled the postwar confusion of Los Angeles with his wife and three daughters, seeking a more relaxed, natural life. He leased the land surrounding Giant Rock and constructed a dirt airstrip, catering to the needs of weekend fliers visiting the desert and servicing small airplanes. Living and working in the desert solitude, Van Tassel gradually became aware of his gift for telepathy and ESP. The commercial development of Giant Rock became less important as he began to practice a daily regimen of nonverbal communication. A large grotto beneath the mass of Giant Rock, the hideaway of a German spy during World War II, served as Van Tassel's meditation chamber.

"My whole body was shaken up when the Council of Seven Lights came through," wrote the fifty-year-old Van Tassel of his first contact with the space beings in 1951. Ashtar, a commandant of an orbiting space station controlled by the Council of Seven Lights from the planet Shanchea, was the first to talk to Van Tassel. The early contacts with the space beings, Etherians, were sporadic. Then, as the regularity of communications with Ashtar or Zoltan or Desca increased, so did the number of curious observers who had heard of George Van Tassel and came to participate in Saturday night meetings under Giant Rock. Van Tassel soon progressed to initiating contact with the space beings, linking up through "Omnibeam," a kind of outer-space conference call.

Many of those attending Van Tassel's early sessions later became influential in other flying-saucer groups: George Hunt Williamson gained publicity for his work with George Adamski; Bob Short still "channels" for the space beings from his Blue Rose Ministry in Joshua Tree; Gabriel Green attempted through his Amalgamated Flying Saucer Clubs of America to forge a political coalition that could pressure the U.S. government to release its files on flying saucers. Daniel Boone, a construction worker from Santa Barbara, was so impressed by his first meeting, in 1952, that he commuted to Giant Rock every weekend for a year. "He spoke

★

deeply and of great truths," notes Boone. Eventually Boone moved to the desert and subsequently married one of Van Tassel's daughters.

The meetings beneath Giant Rock followed an unchanging procedure. The most intimate followers, the Council of Twelve, would form a ring around Van Tassel, who dictated the seating arrangement. To raise the vibration level of the group they sang popular songs or hymns such as "Sweet Mystery of Life" or "The Old Rugged Cross"; other favorites included songs given to Van Tassel's daughters by the space people. Following a short period of meditation and chanting of "Peace—Love—Harmony," Van Tassel would await contact.

"Yes, we are here. Who am I talking to?" asks Van Tassel in one recorded session. Apparently the space people often experienced difficulty in adjusting the Omnibeam. "NOW who am I talking to? CONFOUND IT! YOU KEEP SWITCHING AROUND ON ME! Let's settle on who is to do the talking tonight!" Suddenly, a harsh voice from Van Tassel's throat, "I AM KNUT. I BRING YOU LOVE."

The space beings couched their messages in the cloying reasonableness and veiled threats of a propaganda broadcast: "Through the control of light forces we can instantly terminate production, transportation and communication at any time, at any place upon your planet. Our laws do not permit us to take human life. They do not, however, forbid us to control minds. . . . This is a friendly warning."

The space beings brought word of the higher forms of life and power in the outer strata of the cosmos, including the moon. Extensive information about the positive and negative electrical forces of Creation was laid out with mechanical exactness. Other revelations communicated by the space beings shed new light on such biblical phenomena as the Star of Bethlehem, Ezekiel's wheel within a wheel, and the Tabernacle of Moses. Transcripts of the communications were reprinted in *Proceedings,* the organ of Van Tassel's newly founded Ministry of Universal Wisdom Inc.

On the night of August 24, 1953, Van Tassel awoke to find a man standing near the foot of his bed. "I am Solganda," the slight figure announced, "I would be pleased to show you our craft." A hundred yards away, a glowing spaceship hovered several feet off the ground, glittering in the light of a full moon. Solganda showed Van Tassel the craft's interior of shimmering mother-of-pearl panels and demonstrated its instruments and mode of propulsion. Solganda also revealed that people exist everywhere in the Creator's universe. "Most of them have followed the universal laws and progressed," Solganda noted, "while Earthlings experiment with new ways to destroy millions of their fellow beings." Writing in *Proceedings,* Van Tassel explained: "When one of their people gets destructive ideas they isolate that one and place him on a planet. It looks like this is the planet." Nuclear testing in particular was creating havoc on many life levels, and flying saucers, the "signs in the sky" referred to in the Bible, had been dispatched to monitor the problems on Earth.

Van Tassel also learned from the space beings that "The biggest difficulties in our Earth's progression was our short life span . . . by the time we grow old enough to know how to live, we die." The space beings determined that in order to pull Earth out of its karmic morass they would have to extend the life cycle of humans to give us enough time to "get it right." Solganda revealed to Van Tassel through thought communication the detailed plans for constructing the Integratron, a device that would add years to human life and offer an opportunity to achieve cosmic understanding. "This is not a dream," Van Tassel wrote. "It is a method to a fuller, longer, energetic life for everybody. *Let one generation live* to correct its own mistakes!"

The plans transmitted to Van Tassel called for an electro-static magnetic generator to regenerate the cell structure of subjects entering a "time zone" created by "two split fields [with] a common core flux." Despite the seeming complexity of such a machine, Van Tassel claimed that "the principle of operation is ten times simpler than color television." He viewed the Integratron as a "21st Century version of the Tabernacle that Moses constructed" and borrowed heavily from the book of Exodus for details. The "rings" contructed by Moses were extrapolated to mean coils, "staves" became condensers, while "tenons" were interpreted as wires. In place of a covering of goatskins and cloth curtains,

Van Tassel utilized fiberglass and plywood. The gilding for the dome described in Exodus 25:11 found its way into the Integratron as aluminum foil, an inexpensive substitute not available to Moses.

The Integratron represented a complicated technical undertaking and a long-term financial commitment. Initial site plans drawn up in 1954 display a complex of buildings, including a seminary, refectory, swimming pool, and houses for the more devout followers, all cloistered behind a border of acacia and olive trees. "We are ready to 'make you young' soon after our Research Laboratory Building is built and finished," Van Tassel offered readers of *Proceedings*. "You can't take your money with you, but you can live to spend it."

Through appeals in *Proceedings* and later at the spacecraft conventions at Giant Rock, Van Tassel launched a drive for funds to construct the Integratron. He also created a new scientific branch of his ministry, the College of Universal Wisdom, and his initial request, in 1955, to his followers at the college was for $45,000 to make the Integratron operational within two or three years. "Man in space is free," wrote Van Tassel. "The limits of human confinement in the prison of flesh can be escaped by knowledge of the immutable laws of the Creative Spirit and the unselfish application of His scientific principles for others.... Wake up! You vertical dead who amass fortunes for the devil to enslave you with. The rest of this secret of the cross is awaiting your awakening." Van Tassel also offered the resumption of youthful vitality to the wealthy in exchange for substantial donations.

"Think about it, some of you tired-out millionaire playboys!" Indeed, one source told me of several occasions when chauffered black limousines made late night calls to the Integratron.

Work progressed slowly on the Integratron, but by 1959 a dome-topped building had risen from the desert floor. Fifty-five feet in diameter and four storeys high, it was constructed entirely without nails, screws, or any part of iron or steel. A report in the June 1961 *Proceedings* forecast the need for additional funds and two to three more years to complete the functioning parts for the rejuvenator. It noted that further benefits of the machine, including antigravity forces and time travel, had presented themselves in preliminary studies.

Van Tassel reported in 1975 that eighty-eight percent of the work was completed and promised the imminent functioning of the generator. Throughout this period contradictory rumors about the Integratron circulated throughout the flying-saucer community. Some sources had it that the monies for the project were held by Van Tassel in a numbered Swiss bank acount, while others talked of his suffering from malnutrition in order to keep the dream alive. Work on the Integratron was accomplished primarily by Van Tassel, assisted by his sons-in-law, Dan Boone and Edwin Wrenchey, both directors of the college. "He was alway pretty limited on the financial end of it," says Dan of his father-in-law. "It was always a hardship for all of us there. He was a dedicated, sacrificial type. Any extra bucks any of us made went into the project. So it was a hard grind for 25 years—that's why George started writing books and planning lectures, trying to raise interest and donations."

Throughout these trials, Giant Rock with its "natural receptivity" and annual conventions, remained a Mecca for believers. If the Integratron was the modern version of the Tabernacle, then it was apparent that Van Tassel would be a suitable stand-in for Moses, and indeed he believed that a future chapter in the Bible would be written about him.

Van Tassel died suddenly in 1978, never seeing his ambitions fulfilled. His epitaph was fittingly communicated by a space being named Lo: "Birth through Induction ... Death through Short Circuit."

After Van Tassel's death, his widow, Doris, continued to operate the College of Universal Wisdom and to publish *Proceedings*. Under financial pressure from county tax authorities, she sold the property in 1979 to Jimmy Velasquez, a San Diego developer who subsequently revealed his intention to turn the Integratron into a discothèque. Former followers of Van Tassel rallied and bought the land back in 1981. Edwin Wrenchey and Dan Boone make sure that a fresh coat of paint is applied to the dome each year and await the funds needed to make the machine operative.

John Shepherd has converted his
grandparent's home into a UFO-
detecting station. Bellaire, Michigan.

In John Shepherd's front yard, partially obscured by a stand of blue spruce, stands a ten-foot tower surmounted by antennae, speakers, and small blue lights blinking in sequence to the chirping of what sounds like twenty electronic canaries. Wind off the nearby lake gusts through the spruce and mingles with the electronic chaff being blown off into the ionosphere.

If he is home, John's voice will boom out at you, echoing in lag from speakers hidden in the surrounding evergreens. If he's not, then his grandmother, Mrs. Lamb, will likely beckon you inside.

The house is small and carries the smell of wood smoke. You enter by the dining room, which is dominated by an oilclothed table and an upright piano. To your left, in the farm kitchen, tea towels dry on a line stretched over the woodstove. Ahead, the room opens onto the living room and a fieldstone fireplace. A game show flickers on the television. To the right, phosphorescent loops, squiggling test patterns, and blinking lights float in a black void beyond a large plate-glass window. Though muted by the thick glass, the sound accompaniment to the gyrating, pulsing electronics still competes with the television in the living room beyond.

John is trying to contact extraterrestrial life. For years now, each morning at ten he has begun broadcasting music and binary signals from Earth Station Radio. The music and signals pulse from a home-built twenty-foot transmitter accelerator assembly sunk into the bowels of his facility. From jazz to rock to African tribal rhythms, John chooses music he feels to be uplifting, encompassing "true artistic human energy." "The point of this is to broadcast the human species—the energy within, as a being, a creative entity. It's important to express that, not just to put anything out there."

John's station has been in operation for nearly eleven years, constantly changing and growing in sophistication. In a black pit in the center of the room are sunk large hydro transformers scrounged from the local power utility, looped and crossed by heavy cables. Rising out of this well is the accelerator tower, a structure reminiscent of an Edison experiment. Plates and grids bracketed with insulators set up a fierce buzzing as the signal charge crosses over them in a fan of blue arcs into the antennae. The saturated magnetic field ionizes the air, leaving the smell of ozone as after a lightning storm.

Underfoot and along the baseboards run cable bundles the thickness of a man's arm, while overhead hang service boards and modules mounted with UV meters, phase loop converters, signal-strength indicators, manometers, voltmeters, pulse shapers, pulse-shape monitors, potentiometers, switches, patch cords, ICs, LEDs, and ready lights. All of it alive and talking to itself and someone or something, immeasurable miles and galaxies away.

Coupled with the signaling gear is a system for detecting UFOs. In operation twenty-four hours a day, gravimeters monitor any violent changes in the Earth's magnetic field caused by UFOs. Radio direction–finding gear, coupled with the gravimeters, would attempt to pinpoint such a disturbance and in turn trigger a prerecorded message of peace and goodwill interspersed with binary tone signals automatically ranged over a scale of frequencies by a signal scanner.

"The idea is to find a straightforward approach to transmitting electromagnetic energy similar to what their devices seem to pick up on. The idea is to get them into the test tube where you can analyze them."

Obviously, such equipment as John possesses is not available through Radio Shack catalogs. For John, the search for extraterrestrial life and the need to acquire the necessary technical skills have required considerable time and dedication. He grew up in Detroit. At the age of thirteen, while stripping apart a broken radio, he glanced up to catch sight of unexplained lights overhead. This occurred during the mid-1960s UFO flap over Detroit, the same upsurge in sightings that was to draw Charles Gaiffe from spiritualist meetings into UFO circles and eventually to work on the Bluebird flying saucer (see pages 88–94). When John's family split and his mother remarried, he came to live with his grandparents in their small house on the shore of Intermediate Lake. By the time he was fifteen, he was repairing radios. Dissatisfied with

school, he dropped out and began souping up sound equipment for local rock bands.

John and his grandma live frugally; for example, they do without natural gas service in order to funnel money into materials for the project. Grandpa Lamb used to grumble at the growing incursion of paraphernalia into the living room. Eventually, he and Mrs. Lamb were left with only a small settee scrunched into a corner between whole walls taken up by John's consoles and oscilloscopes. Grandpa Lamb died two years ago. Now John and his grandmother make a good team. Together they built an addition on the house to allow space for John's burgeoning equipment and put a rocking chair in the living room for Mrs. Lamb.

Local people have undergone a marked change in their attitude toward John and his work in the last few years. Previously he was regarded as a crank, but with the exposure he and his work have received on television and in publications such as the *National Enquirer*, people now speak of him with open respect. From the local newspaper to shopkeepers to the mechanic at the corner Union 76, all express admiration for John and exhibit a "George Washington slept here" pride in his living in their community—an attitude shared even by the local state police, who might have reason to view John's work otherwise.

One night, a state patrolman radioed for help—a flying saucer had landed in a nearby wood. Squad cars raced to the scene, sirens wailing. Guns drawn, the police advanced into the woods toward the mysterious object—blinking lights and blurping electronic whoops. The "flying saucer" proved to be one of John Shepherd's remote UFO-detectors, triggered by the state trooper's relieving himself in the bushes.

As John and I walked through town, people stopped him to ask him how he was doing, what new improvements he was working on. A teenager in a wrestling team jacket asked if John could fix his tape deck. A lineman with the local utility, which often calls upon John's troubleshooting ability, offered him a length of scrap wire.

If there are other intelligent beings somewhere out there in the cosmos—and John believes there are—they have not yet sent back a signal. Twenty-four hours a day he leaves on the receiving sensors, the high- and low-frequency scanners. Throughout the days, the music goes out, interspersed with binary code.

For John, the correlation between events is never coincidental. There is an unseen order of things, though he hesitates to term it God's will. He views many events as portentous:

seeing the lights in the sky while probing a broken radio for the first time; the insatiable public appetite for films involving extraterrestrials; even my arrival on his doorstep. During our talks, he said: "There's definitely a purpose ... a plan of some kind ... people are being prepared. People are being affected psychologically, sociologically. In this realm, this subject, this UFO thing is different from normal life patterns.... I've been doing this work for approximately fourteen years and building these things, all by hand, constructing this project and trying to evaluate the creative effort to search."

When you walk into John's room at night, all the instruments are humming softly, in inky blackness, just lights switching on and off, and soft sounds. The air smells of transistors. It's peaceful and reassuring. It feels reliable and as if it will go on forever. Often John will go in there by himself and sit late into the night, looking at the lights and listening to the transformers hum.

Space Age Lodge. Gila Bend, Arizona.

This motel and a more extreme version of it just a block from Disneyland in Anaheim, California, were opened by Leo Stovall in 1965 and are known as Stovall's Space Age Lodges. A plaque above the Anaheim registration desk reads:

On behalf of the Stovall's, we take great pride in presenting a new motel concept and creation, The Space Age Lodge, for your comfort and luxury while you're at Disneyland and the Magic Kingdom.

The Space Bubble dividers, new styrene lights and panels, grape plaques, bubble mirrors and lights, fallout detectors, new acetate spreads and drapes with exciting new colors make *The Space Age Lodge* the pacesetter for motels in the future.

These creations along with the geometric trim, thousands of space spheres combined with aluminum and *jet-age metals* on stairs, railings, pool, and atrium, all made by the Stovalls to make this your best and most memorable vacation.

The dining room, used by the Rotarians for weekly luncheons, features a wall-length photo mural of Earth seen from outer space. Parabolas of aircraft-tubing arch over the front portico, and merry spacemen prance along the eaves overlooking the parking lot, with satellites stuck to the roof like cockleburrs. Perforated waferlike aluminum, a metallic Swiss cheese, encases the banisters and railings. A sign on the geodesic dome sheltering ice and Coke machines out by the swimming pool boasts that the structure is a replica of the first building erected on the moon. Framed pictures of planets and moon photographs are mounted above the beds in each room, while red and orange planetlike globes hang in corners and along the windows.

The motels were recently bought by the Best Western chain, and the new owners have toned down the more unusual aspects of Leo's decorative scheme.

Charles Gaiffe with the mold for
the propulsion unit for the Bluebird
flying saucer. Toledo, Ohio.

I met Charles Gaiffe in November 1977 at Giant Rock, California, the site of the Annual Interplanetary Spacecraft Convention. Charles, an energetic seventy-eight-year old, had driven out alone from his home in Ohio to seek advice from UFO contactee George Van Tassel, creator of the Integratron and owner of the Giant Rock Airport (see pages 79–81). Charles and I spent the night around his campfire, talking and eating grapefruit. Before I headed off to sleep in my car, he handed me a note addressed to a man in Detour Village, on the Upper Peninsula of Michigan. "Dear Ed," the note read, "please allow this nice young man to view the saucer and oblige him as possible. Signed, Charles Gaiffe."

It was over two years later that I arrived on Ed Kelcheski's doorstep with Charles's note in hand. Ed pulled on a coat and instructed me to follow him to the hangar, a short drive away. He opened the hangar door and light streamed in to reveal the saucer sitting on blocks. Pieces of wood, steel, and machinery for the ship lay scattered across the floor and Kelcheski walked in small circles around the pile of debris. Tears welling in his eyes, he looked around the disheveled hangar. "It hurts to see this you know. There's so many dreams tied up in all of this."

The Advanced Scientific Development Project (ASDP) was formed in 1967 as a nonprofit organization under the directorship of Warren Goetz, the son of a wealthy Upper Peninsula family. Goetz alleged that he was the product of spontaneous birth: one day a flying saucer appeared over his parents' home and Warren suddenly appeared in his mother's lap, wrapped in white muslin. Later, Goetz would imply to favored members of the group that he was reincarnated from Io (one of the moons of Jupiter) and had been sent by the Space Brothers to fulfill a mission. Goetz also claimed that during World War II he had served as a communications specialist and later as one of the first American researchers on the captured German V-2 rockets.

During the late 1950s Goetz became involved, along with Wayne Aho, in promoting Otis T. Carr's ill-fated OTC-X1, "a four-dimensional saucer that was to be, at one and the same time, completely round and completely square." Carr offered the ship to the military in 1958 for $20,000,000 but was refused. In April 1959 a planned demonstration of a six-foot model in Oklahoma City ended in failure but Carr, undaunted, stated that he and Aho would "fly to the moon in a flying saucer on December 7, 1959." Shortly after the failed liftoff attempt in April, the prototype mysteriously burned in its warehouse and all of the "three-dimensional" plans disappeared. Aho returned to the Pacific Northwest and formed the New Age Foundation (see pages 50–55), Goetz headed to Michigan to begin "counseling," and Carr sank to obscurity in a slum tenement in Pittsburg. Goetz later told an ASDP member that he himself had destroyed the prototype under guidance from the Space Brothers, who told him that Carr was working in a negative manner by being too capitalistic with what was meant to be a gift to the world.

Goetz became known throughout Michigan and Ohio, lecturing on metaphysics and flying saucers. At one of his talks in 1965 he spoke about building a two-man flying saucer in the basement of his house. Members of the audience asked if they could help. Goetz thought this was a possibility, provided that the Space Brothers did not object, and the Advanced Scientific Development Project was begun. Goetz articulated the goals of the ASDP in an early newsletter: "to build a full-scale working model of a Venusian-type saucer capable of manned flight, and, to get people to live Love and Truth and Universal Law through an understanding of the Almighty and the workings of his creation."

The flying saucer was christened the Bluebird, in reference to a Hopi myth. (The Hopi Indians believed that their ancestors had come to earth from the red planet in the Bluebird, a vehicle resembling a flying saucer.) Goetz told members of the group:

The flying saucer must be built so it can lead spaceships from all the planets in the solar system as they fly over the Earth. There will be so many that they will block out the sun and it will be dark for three days. People will look up and wonder why. They will want to know how to build their own flying saucers. In order to do this they will first have to learn Universal Law, and will seek out members of the ASDP to teach it to them.

Charles Gaiffe was an original member of the Advanced Scientific Development Project. A retired screw-machine operator and machinist, he was to become a core member of the group, one of those who combined the necessary qualities of faith and skill. Charles believed that during the war he had unwittingly helped to machine parts that were subsequently used in the atomic bomb, and he recognized the ASDP project as a way to reconcile himself with God for this inadvertent sin. Soon after hearing Goetz talk in Toledo, Charles bought a piece of land from Goetz and turned it over to the ASDP as the site for the Bluebird's hangar.

Another member, Roger (not his real name), who was to become second-in-command of the project, heard about the flying saucer through the Rosicrucians. According to one report, when he saw the cab of the flying saucer under construction in Goetz's basement Roger immediately recognized it as the same machine that he had dreamed he had been sent to Earth to build. As part-owner of an industrial repair shop in Detroit, Roger was able to supply tools and materials needed on the project.

Most of the members came from the Detroit-Toledo area, though some were from as far away as New Jersey and Canada. They ranged in occupation from salesman to carpenter, housewife to high school student, including a lay preacher and an ex-nun. Within the group a subtle hierarchy developed: those closest to Goetz, whose skills were essential to the advancement of the saucer; those of limited skills who could help; and those primarily interested in Goetz's teachings of Universal Law. For some members Goetz was a source for cures, and at least one viewed him as a manifestation of God. From time to time skilled outsiders were brought in to perform specific functions and were subsequently induced to become members. Others simply arrived at the work site and, vouched for by another member, began working. Eventually many members purchased lots on the surrounding land from Goetz and moved in trailers to live in during work periods. Several members, some with families, moved permanently to the Upper Peninsula to be nearer the project and Goetz. Although some of these members worked on the saucer throughout the week, activity was concentrated on the weekends. For most people, working on the Bluebird required a six-hundred-mile round-trip, and some made the journey only once or twice during the summer. Dedicated members such as Roger attended every weekend from spring through fall as well as vacation time, often at the expense of their families and jobs.

Members arriving late on a Friday evening for a weekend of work would report to Goetz's home. Sitting at the kitchen table with his wife, Goetz would talk into the morning hours, discussing the latest developments on the saucer, explaining aspects of Universal Law, and telling anecdotes about other members. On Saturday evenings, after a day's work inside the hangar, members could often glance up into the clear Michigan night skies and see friendly flying saucers hovering overhead. Then they would again converge around the kitchen table, drinking coffee and talking about karma, reincarnation, or harnessing "lines of force" for the saucer motor. Prayer sessions were held at nine o'clock: hymns would be sung or group members would pray for the sick by "outpicturing" them as healed in the minds of group members. On special occasions Goetz would read a prepared talk or recite poems about the flying saucer to the group.

From time to time Goetz would reveal certain artifacts to the core technicians on the project. A small red plastic disk with winking lights, which he claimed ran on free energy, was presented for scrutiny, as well as photographs of small flying saucers whipping around his basement laboratory. (He maintained that one small saucer flew out of sight and was later returned by the space people.) These models were based on photographs of Venusian scout ships made many years earlier by George Adamski. Goetz also produced a large cylindrical crystal sapphire, given to him by the space people, which was to be the catalyst for the Bluebird's free-energy motor.

Goetz and Roger together directed most of the work on the saucer. Blueprints were never in evidence since the space people had conveyed much of the information to Goetz telepathically so that it couldn't fall into the wrong hands. Goetz had a general idea of how to construct the saucer, but the details were often worked out by the technicians. "I told them what to make, and about how, and they made it professionally," Goetz said during a 1971 ASDP meeting. Roger was called on to solve the most difficult problems, such as how to construct an elaborate transmission and roller assembly that would allow the large outer skirt of the saucer to rotate at great speed in the direction opposite to the inner passenger cabin and power assembly. He arrived at his solutions by sitting and meditating, reaching out into the "lines of force" of the universe to grasp the solutions.

Approximately thirty-five feet in diameter, the Bluebird was made entirely of nonferrous materials. Marine plywood, fiberglass, and copper form most of the construction, while vital components such as the transmission were built with aluminum alloys and aerospace metals. The planetary gear transmission, three feet in diameter, was valued by some members at over $100,000. Gus Hebel, the owner of the precision shop where the transmission was machined, recently wrote: "I, personally, do not regret any time or money spent with Warren's 'project' as do some of the others. This involvement opened ways to new visions which within the next 500 years will be a reality."

The saucer was to be run by a "double-vortex" engine, which would harness the energy latent in the "lines of force" that powered the universe. The "vortex" was a swirling mass existing between the lines of force. The double-vortex motor would manipulate positive and negative forces to produce a weightless condition: the forces "would exceed the pull of the earth's magnetism and move the [Bluebird] out into space."

Work proceeded slowly but steadily until 1977, when a number of circumstances combined to ground the Bluebird forever. As the saucer neared completion, the problem of exactly how to convert free energy into mechanical energy to spin the saucer grew pressing. Goetz began to stall on designing the components needed to link the still-undeveloped power unit to the existing structure. Frustrated by the lack of progress, Roger made a trip to Pittsburg and sought out the ailing Otis Carr, who told him about the missing plans for the OTC-X1 and its obvious similarities to the Bluebird. In the meantime, Goetz had issued a communication from the space people about a galactic war between the people of Io and Pluto. The Plutonians were known within the ASDP cosmology to be scientifically advanced but spiritually negative beings; since they had triumphed, work on the Bluebird would have to end to prevent its falling into their dangerous hands. Goetz finally shattered the confidence of most of the group by getting involved with a young woman who had recently joined ASDP. Charles spoke for most of the membership when he told me of Goetz's downfall, "He was led astray by his sex glands."

Goetz severed his ties with the ASDP later in 1977 and established a school for the teaching of Universal Law. In the first newsletter for his School of Evolvement, Goetz summarily dismissed the ten years of work on the Bluebird. "The Advanced Scientific Development Project has been discontinued. Our period of research is complete. We have positive proof of the Laws of the Universe—both of science and of religion. Now we

The Bluebird sits in a barn in northern
Michigan. Detour Village, Michigan.

build—with absolute confidence—a cohesive School of Evolvement for the Great Intelligence."

A legal battle followed the dissolution of the ASDP. Members sought to regain tools, materials, or, as in Charles Gaiffe's case, the property and hangar where the Bluebird was stored. Charles remained determined to see the ship fly, and it was for this reason that he had gone to Giant Rock, California, to meet George Van Tassel. Although Van Tassel's Integratron was considered to be based on many of the same principles of magnetism determined with guidance from the space people, Van Tassel was unable to provide Charles with any surefire technology. Disappointed but undaunted, Charles returned home to his small tool shed in Toledo, intent on building a free-energy motor.

Whenever I travel east I make a point of stopping in to see Charles. Peering through the window of his shop out behind his house, I might find him sitting in a wired-together swivel chair, contemplating a machined part, or hunched over the lathe with curls of copper splitting off a new turning. For Charles, the motor, the purpose of his life, and God's will are inextricably tied together. He believes that guardian angels watch over him and that God keeps him alive as long as he works on the motor. The more complex parts of his invention are still made for him in the shops of old friends who long ago deserted the dream of the Bluebird.

Control panel for the Bluebird. Switch labels include "Viscorator," "High Flow Throttle," and "Gravity Tester." Detour Village, Michigan.

The UFO house at Pensacola Beach.
Pensacola, Florida.
These flying-saucer–inspired modular
homes, thirty-six feet in diameter,
were marketed by a now-defunct
California company under the name
Future Fiberglass Homes. I have also
found them serving as a private home
in rural Quebec, a real estate office
in Dallas, and a striptease joint in
Tampa.

On any Saturday morning at the Weslaco flea market the air is hazed with dust and gasoline fumes. Mariachi music blares out from speakers, echoing over the tables of used tools, second-hand clothing, and mounds of cheap sunglasses and car stereos smuggled over the Mexican border a few miles to the south.

O. T. Nodrog can be found setting up his table and wares under the sheltering palm trees. He is known locally for producing good avocado plants, and many of these, as well as jars of wheat berries and honey, are set out in small cans and used yogurt containers all around his selling area. In the center of the table, held down against the wind by a rock, is a stack of leaflets. "WANTED! REAL MEN, REAL WOMEN," proclaims the flyer. "Real Human Beings! Positive Pioneers Who are Capable of Facing the Reality of The Time Frontier and Redeveloping and Repopulating of the Manasseh Complex. *Study* and *Act* upon our *Standing Offer of Proof.*"

A battered three-quarter-ton pickup, its box piled high with used furniture, tires, and a child's tricycle, is parked next to Nodrog's stand. The owner of the truck, Fred Holt, has lived at Nodrog's Armageddon Time Ark Base, along with his wife and five children, since 1975. A grizzled man with a square-set jaw and a deep Kentucky accent, Holt had been laid off his job as a lumber cutter in Oregon and drifted south with his family, eventually meeting Nodrog at the flea market.

"When we set down and started to readin' the Bible after we met him, we could find everthin' in there, man. Just seemed like a *revelation* opened up to us," explained Fred. "Whole thing to us was *real* that he was talking about." Holt reaches into the cab of the truck and pulls a dusty Bible from its place on the dashboard. "Y'ever read Isaiah 66:15? 'For, behold the Lord will come with fire, and with his chariots like a whirlwind, to render his anger with fury, and his rebuke with flames of fire.'" Snapping the Bible shut, Holt gestures over to Nodrog, who is making change for a customer buying an avocado plant in a rusty coffee can. "This is the double-edged sword of God—*right here.* And he is *pleadin'* with *all* the flesh."

Followers of the ODF point to the Bible for substantiation of their ideas, which they call "perfect facts." They hold the Bible to be factual history, although it's been "perverfraction-eered" by those of the negative birthright to serve the manipulative purposes of traditional religion. They view Earth as Time Station Earth, a temporary entity consisting of only three and a half dimensions. Present-day America, called the "Manasseh Complex" after the lands held by one of the ten lost tribes of ancient Israel, has been turned from its path of righteousness by the deceit of the government and the perversion of the church, which ODF followers call, respectively, The Beast and The Harlot.

The Outer Dimensional Forces (ODF) channel the opportunity for surviving S-Day through Nodrog and members of his group at the Armageddon Time Ark Base. Weslaco, Texas.

★

★

Nodrog and the ODF seek individuals who have sufficiently removed themselves from this negative system to help prepare for one thousand years of rule by the Creator, Yahweh. Yahweh alternates one-thousand-year periods of his rule with stretches of six thousand years during which man is granted free moral agency. At the conclusion of the six-thousand-year "dispensation," he makes his power known through the appearance in the skies of his Time Ark Service Modules. Mistakenly referred to as the "cloud" and the "pillar of fire" in Exodus and as UFOs today, these are actually five-dimensional starships commanded by the son of Yahweh, Yahshua Hamashiia. The Service Modules cruise the universe awaiting S-Day, when Yahweh activates the Sixth Seal of Revelations.

On the evening before S-Day the skies will "roll back as a scroll," and the entire fleet of Service Modules will "funcionate interdimensional power exchange." Within minutes, all airplanes will crash to the ground. Only those who have "kept their lamps filled with oil" and completed their Survival Training through the Armageddon Time Ark Base will be evacuated aboard smaller versions of the starships. Early on the morning of S-Day the cosmic fleet will effect a six-degree shift in the Earth's polar alignment. The Manasseh Complex, shuddering and convulsing, will move eastward as earthquakes crack open the land and the seas inundate the continent. To the west of present-day Weslaco will arise a new mountain, draining off the flooded valley of the lower Rio Grande. This valley will be the new Eden, the City Foursquare envisioned in Revelations 21:16, a new home for the ten lost tribes of the Positive Birthright. The survivors aboard the rescue ships will be landed on this new Manasseh Free Territory. In addition to receiving a "hide of land," manna, and a Mini-Star version of the starship with a thousand-year guarantee, each family unit will have the opportunity to earn a living free of government parasitism.

"For that 1% of the population which is up to the demands of facing the time frontier" the ODF offers training in the operation of a 13,000-mile-per-hour 4 D.O.—the junior starship that will evacuate followers before S-Day. Admission to the "1%" is determined by the staff after submission of a completed "Procedural Instructions" form and a $25 fee. The members being sought are those exhibiting what would popularly be thought of as "American values": "The competency, the productivity, the self-determination, and the self-sufficiency to be on the winning side. We do not accept parasites."

My first knowledge of O. T. Nodrog came through John Schuessler, a NASA engineer working on the space shuttle program in Houston. Schuessler has devoted much of his spare time to studying possible modes of UFO propulsion, and he is a founding member of MUFON (Mutual UFO Network), an international reporting-investigating organization seeking to understand the phenomenon of flying saucers.

In June 1976 a large manila envelope landed on Schuessler's desk. Postmarked Weslaco, Texas, it featured a logo of an elliptical spaceship with portholes and a glowing command bubble on top. "5 D.O. Power!" the message boasted, "YOUR SURVIVAL SERVICE MODULE. Try us, you may like us." Below the salutation "Ultimitory of greetings" were listed twelve clauses citing charges to be brought against Schuessler and MUFON in the name of Commander Yahshua Hamashiia of the Positive Section of the Outer Dimensional Forces. Accusing Schuessler of willful ignorance and refusing to recognize the efforts of the ODF to "stir you to positive action," the letter offered him the opportunity to surrender at the Armageddon Time Ark Base before the morning of July 4. Surrender, Nodrog pointed out, would "let us help you to shift the fulcrum of your intellect to embrace the full 5 dimensions allotted by your Creator."

Schuessler ignored the charges until a month later, when he received another package with the now-familiar logo. "War Crime 7—A Decree of Judgement" found Schuessler and MUFON guilty of "Suppressing the good news on the return of Time Station Earth's Service Modules." It was the threatening tone, more than the hitherto unheard of cosmic order, that compelled Schuessler to turn the material over to federal postal inspectors and the FBI.

FBI agents followed through on Schuessler's complaint at the wire gate that bars the entrance to the Armageddon Time Ark Base, and as the agents have returned there over the years in response to other complaints these wire-gate powwows have developed their own rituals. The FBI men and the postal inspectors read their charges of abuse of federal statutes to Nodrog or to the Governor of Security, and then they dutifully listen to the litany of perfect facts from the ODF's Cosmic Corps of Engineers. Soon the agents beat a dusty retreat to the welcome familiarity of their district office.

Local information concerning Nodrog and his group is difficult to come by. Orville T. Gordon arrived in Weslaco from Wisconsin in the late 1930s and for years ran a small lumberyard at the site of the present Armageddon Time Ark Base. During the early 1960s he became involved in disputes with local and federal authorities over taxes and closed down the business. In 1963 Yahshua Hamashiia assigned the task of Earth Co-ordinator to Nodrog. When Hurricane Beulah swept the Gulf Coast in 1967, it was seen by Nodrog to be the whirlwind of Christ described in Isaiah 66:15, confirming his mission. Since that time he has continued "pleading with all the flesh" from his Saturday stand at the flea market, slowly building his flock for the advent of S-Day.

In a recent letter to me Nodrog emphasized that "A.T.A. Base Operation is not interested in U.F.O.s, but rather, involved in I.S.O.s (Identified Sailing Objects) which are perfect factual Time Ark Service Modules for Time Station Earth. Please point this out to the readers if you use our information in your book.

"We are becoming quite busy processing late-comers. Several caravans have recently arrived. Advertising costs alone have run over $7,000 for the last month."

While writing this piece I telephoned Daniel Hoverson, Governor of Public Relations, to clarify a detail. "We don't give interviews," Hoverson answered curtly. I protested, citing the interviews and materials freely handed out during my visit to Weslaco in 1982. "You have all the facts you need," he countered. "You've gone back to the Empire."

*

*

*

*

★

Curtis W. King's flying-saucer house.
Signal Mountain, near Chattanooga,
Tennessee.

Radio traffic reports in Chattanooga usually warn commuters to "Watch for slow moving traffic near the flying saucer." The forty-five foot "saucer" faces a short open stretch of the serpentine highway that climbs Signal Mountain, and more than one late-running commuter has barreled around the hairpin turns to find an out-of-town driver transfixed in the middle of the road.

Curtis W. King, creator of the house, can usually be found playing gin rummy in the back of the B&B general store at the foot of Signal Mountain. A concrete contractor by trade, he built the house in 1973 as a "bachelor pad" for his son, but then, because of the $250,000 cost, could not afford to give it to him. The steel and concrete structure is the sturdiest he has ever built, King says. "I believe it could withstand a 200-mile-per-hour hurricane." Many features of flying saucers were incorporated into the design of the house: the retractable stairway ensures privacy, and all the interior rooms are round. "The windows are made of acrylic rather than glass to maintain that spaceship feeling," King noted.

David Graham, the present owner, is enthusiastic about his saucer home: "It's definitely a weird home because it was designed to look like something from another planet. . . . But I love the house. It's modern, 20th century, convenient, and private."

Flying saucer by Jene Highstein, 1980.
Park Forest, Illinois.

Rocket. Topeka, Kansas.

Rocket at Welch's Mountain Fantasy.
Prescott, Arizona.

Ray Welch, an energetic seventy-eight-year-old retired industrialist, opened Welch's Mountain Fantasy in 1979. The centerpiece of his operation—which includes a miniature railway and a man-made musical geyser—is a 1940s science fiction movie rocket. Originally built as a prop for Republic Pictures' *Tibor the Great,* the forty-foot sheet-metal rocket was sold in 1954 to Blakely Oil Company of Phoenix, Arizona. The hull was mounted on a flatbed trailer and the interior was renovated with air conditioning, a twenty-four seat 16mm theater, and a vibrator to simulate space flight. During its stint with Blakely Oil the rocket was carted around from gas station to gas station, where it would entertain kids and adults with an animated space flight movie, realistic rumbling vibrations, and a blinking control panel.

In the mid-1960s the Blakely stations with their rocket-emblazoned signs began to disappear from the desert landscape, and the rocket was sold again, this time to a meat-packing company. Welch bought the rocket in the early 1970s, intending to refurbish it for his amusement park, complete with two midgets with their skin painted green to act as hosts. He commissioned a new $15,000 space flight film and set about repairing the rusting metal skin. On the afternoon I visited him, Welch invited me to a private screening. After securing the hatchway doors, he bounded into a front row seat and sat weaving and ducking as meteors and planets whooshed by us in near misses on the screen.

Jesus appeared to Al Thomas in
1973 and commanded him to build a
flying saucer with which to distribute
food, medicine, and the Bible.
Russellville, Arkansas.

Al Thomas is leaning back in a swivel chair on the concrete apron of his two-bay garage in Russellville. "The *lust* is nothing but *money.* Lust, Lust, LUST! This soil—the trees ain't sinned. The cows and the deer ain't, the butterfly or the bees. The world's sacred—it's man and woman's defiled it." He sweeps his arm back and forth at the traffic passing on the two-lane blacktop as if to rub it out of the world. "Man! It's amazing to me that God puts up with all this."

In a cinder-block hangar at the rear of the garage sits Thomas's unfinished flying saucer. On a plywood panel behind the saucer is written the legend: "Jesus came to Earth on a cloud 6:30 AM, 1973, at Centerville, Arkansas." Jesus appeared to Thomas on a hill and commanded him to circle the Earth in a flying saucer, distributing food, medicine, and the Bible. "He went up in a cloud and he comes back likewise," Thomas advised me. Soon after the encounter Thomas began construction of his saucer, drawing on his mechanical abilities and the books of Ezekiel and Revelations from the Bible. The sheet stainless steel for the outer skin came from a scrap yard in Little Rock, where Thomas brought the morning's work to a halt by preaching to the workers from a mound of scrap iron. The free-energy motor for the saucer, a mass of copper windings around a ceramic core, is under development while Thomas continues his research from a dictionary and the Bible propped up on the workbench beneath a window.

"I was saying to the wife, 'You can have chemistry, history, carbon arc welding, but when you get into the Bible you got all that beat.'

"When this thing starts happening, man! They say, 'Oh, we're gonna fly away! We're going to meet Jesus, we're going to Heaven.' Now these people got the idea Heaven is in outer space—well, it is now—but it's coming to Earth!"

Bob Dunbar wants to train people to fly rockets to outer space. Canaan, Maine.

Bob Dunbar believes that NASA (National Aeronautics and Space Administration) is not training enough people to fly rockets. The dangers of nuclear war, pollution, and overcrowding have made Earth a less than ideal place, he believes, and humanity is not prepared for the mass evacuations that would be necessary in the event of a global crisis. "We could have gone to Mars," Dunbar says. "We could have lived there."

Following the 1969 lunar landing, Dunbar, a junior high school teacher, began constructing his own Apollo rocket simulator to train adults and high school students for space flight. The body of the rocket was salvaged from a water tank and topped with a homemade replica of the Apollo capsule large enough for two trainees. At the base of the rocket an oil-furnace blower and loudspeakers were designed to mimic the roar and flames of an actual lift-off. Inside the air-conditioned capsule the Apollo instrument panel was duplicated with over 150 switches, all connected to "Mission Control" located in the nearby barn. Dunbar dismantled an abandoned fire tower and reassembled it beside the rocket to serve as the gantry. Five years and $15,000 after it was begun, the Somerset Field Trip Center, Inc., a nonprofit organization, opened for rocket flight training. The project failed to attract support or money from either NASA or the local school board, and except for a small, devoted group of students, it remains unused.

In Bob Dunbar's living room hangs a large framed and autographed photograph of Neil Armstrong, the first man on the moon. "Pretty good, eh?" Dunbar says, gesturing to the portrait. "Just like having a letter from Christopher Columbus."

Granger Taylor's flying saucer.
Duncan, Vancouver Island, British
Columbia.

Granger Taylor has vanished as if plucked from the face of the earth. Before disappearing one night in November 1980, he pinned a note on his father's bedroom door: "Dear Mother and Father, I have gone away to walk aboard an alien ship, as recurring dreams assured a 42 month interstellar voyage to explore the vast universe, then return. I am leaving behind all my possessions to you as I will no longer require the use of any. Please use the instructions in my will as a guide to help. Love, Granger." On the other side of the note was a contour map of Mount Waterloo, twenty miles west of the Taylors' home in Duncan, British Columbia.

The forty-two months were up in May 1984. Jim and Grace Taylor have left the back door unlocked in case their son shows up. But he never has.

Taylor's shy, self-effacing manner and introspective nature earned the six-foot-three-inch, 240-pound Granger the sobriquet of Gentle Ben. But it was through Granger's exceptional mechanical abilities that he was most known to the logging and fishing community of Duncan. "I guess you could call him an eccentric genius," said longtime friend Bob Nielson. The property surrounding the Taylors' home is strewn with Granger's projects and resurrected machinery: old tractors, donkey engines, an ancient bulldozer, and vintage 1950s Lincolns and Imperials parked beneath rainsheds.

Granger left school in the eighth grade and found work with a neighbor as a mechanic's helper. After a year or so he quit and worked on his own, welding and repairing machinery and vehicles beneath the tall fir trees on his family's land. At fourteen Granger built a one-cylinder car that is now on display at the Duncan Forest Museum, along with a steam locomotive that he hauled out of the bush and restored. At seventeen he overhauled a bulldozer that no one else had been able to repair. He built a replica of a World War II fighter plane that was later sold to a collector for $20,000.

Granger became involved with UFOs in the late 1970s, reading books such as *What We REALLY Know about FLYING SAUCERS, Flying Saucers—Here and Now,* and *The Secret Forces of the Pyramids.* He built his spaceship out of two satellite receiving dishes and outfitted it with a television, a couch, and a wood-burning stove. He became obsessed with finding out how flying saucers were powered, spending hours sitting in the ship thinking and often sleeping there.

A month before he disappeared, Granger told Bob Nielson that he had had a contact with another being. "He lay there and got mental communications with somebody from another galaxy," Nielson recalled. "He couldn't see them ... they were just talking to him and to his mind. He was asking questions about the means for powering their craft. The only thing they would tell him was that it was magnetic." A few days later Granger mentioned that he'd been invited to go on a trip through the solar system. He would know at the end of the month when and where he would be picked up. He prepared two wills for his parents, detailing what they should do with his possessions. The word *deceased* was scratched out and replaced with *departed.*

On the night that Granger disappeared a storm struck the central part of Vancouver Island. Hurricane winds were reported and electrical power was knocked out. Granger vanished, along with his blue pickup truck.

After four years of "exhaustive checks" of hospital, passport, employment, and vehicle records, the Royal Canadian Mounted Police have not uncovered a single clue as to the whereabouts of Granger Taylor. "I can hardly believe Granger's off in a spaceship," his father said. "But if there is a flying object out there, he's the one to find it."

★

John Reeves, "the spaceman of
Brooksville," and his flag from Venus.
Brooksville, Florida.

One afternoon in March 1965, while taking a walk in the scrub flats near his home, a retired longshoreman named John Reeves encountered a silver-suited and helmeted alien being. After advancing to within fifteen feet of where the startled Reeves was crouching behind a bush, the five-foot-tall alien examined him for several minutes, then reached "into his left side" and produced a black object six inches in diameter. The object, raised to about chin height, flashed a brilliant light. Now thoroughly frightened, Reeves turned and ran, looking back only when he was safely behind a tree a hundred yards away. The alien had not moved. It raised the black object again, flashed it, and calmly turned and entered a thirty-foot iridescent spaceship. On the rim of the saucer a series of paddlelike slats began to open and close as the rim started to rotate. A low rumbling turned into a roar and then a whistle as the ship lifted straight up off the palmetto and out of sight.

After the saucer left, Reeves searched the area where it had been. Many footprints shaped roughly like a figure eight were found, as well as impressions from the legs of the saucer. A tightly wadded piece of paper proved to be two thin but exceptionally tough sheets inscribed with a cryptic message of semicircles, dots, and lines. Reeves reported his encounter the following day to reporters at WFFB Radio, who in turn called investigators from nearby MacDill Air Force Base. By that evening the property behind Reeves's home was overrun with curiosity seekers, reporters, and photographers. News of the sighting and the cryptic message spread, and within a week large television caravans with roof-mounted cameras were filming the Air Force investigators sent from Wright-Patterson Field as they measured and triangulated impressions and elevations. The road to Reeves's home was blocked on both sides of the highway, and he conducted a brisk business renting parking spaces at 25¢ per car. The site assumed a festival atmosphere with families picnicking and camping out, hoping for a return of the alien ship.

But the spaceship didn't return. The military cryptographers decoded the message on the papers as: "Planet Mars—Are you coming home soon? We missing you very much," and they declared the sighting a hoax. Reeves subsequently passed a barrage of lie-detector tests. After the crowds and reporters left, he began building a testimonial to the alien. In his front yard he erected a twenty-three-foot obelisk topped with a crescent moon and a replica of Planet Earth. To the west he constructed a large wooden flying saucer, complete with paddlelike vanes. Reeves became known as "the Brooksville spaceman" and started wearing a jumpsuit and erecting cardboard-mounted displays of UFO photographs and news clippings at shopping centers.

In 1968 the aliens visited him again, Reeves said, whisking him away to the moon and Venus (called Moniheya), where he was presented with a Venusian flag. On returning home he expanded his monument to the aliens by erecting a large plaque that read: "The spaceship that took John F. Reeves to planet Moniheya, millions and millions of miles from planet Earth, landed here October 5, 1968."

Harassed by vandals and county tax collectors, Reeves sold his property in 1980 to the state, which razed his house and UFO monument. Letters of protest poured in from throughout Florida objecting to the "desecration of John Reeves's expression of hope." Now eighty-six years old, Reeves lives in a trailer on a side street in Brooksville. His newspaper clippings are kept in an old suitcase that he hauls out for anyone who wants to see. A dog-eared book contains the autographs of people who came to see his UFO monument, among them Jimmy Page of Led Zeppelin, Pat Boone, Tuesday Weld.

Reeves's biggest regret is that he will not be buried in the tomb he had prepared for himself at the foot of the obelisk, which bore this legend:

In this tomb lies the body of John F. Reeves, one of the greatest men of our time, the greatest of them all. Outer space traveller to other planets of our universe.

*

*

*

★

Rocket, built in 1953, on Sepulveda
Boulevard. Los Angeles, California.

Rocket on Main Street.
Sunnyside, Washington.

Alien humanoids, built by George
Rackus. New York, New York.

Betty Andreasson constructed
fiberglass replicas of the aliens who
abducted her aboard a UFO in 1967.
Cheshire, Connecticut.

In 1975 Betty Andreasson read a newspaper article about Dr. J. Allen Hynek and his Center for UFO Studies near Chicago. In the article Hynek made an appeal for reports of unidentified aerial phenomena. Betty wrote to him right away: "Dr. Hynek, I am so happy to read that someone is finally studying about UFOs. Now I can tell someone of my experience ... an encounter in 1967 with UFO occupants." In her letter she sketched the few details she could remember from her January 25 abduction by a group of three-foot-tall humanoids. The experience had come back as visions and flashbacks to haunt her over the years, but she had never been able to discuss it with anyone. Hynek forwarded Betty's letter to the MUFON (Mutual UFO Network) Humanoid Study Group, which was investigating CE IIIs (Close Encounters of the Third Kind).

A MUFON field investigator found that Betty and other members of her family present during the encounter could not remember many aspects of the experience. As with another classic UFO abduction case involving Barney and Betty Hill (described in John Fuller's *The Interrupted Journey*, 1966), the investigators suggested that she undergo hypnotic regression to unlock the memories in her unconscious mind. Between April and July of 1977 Betty underwent fourteen hypnotic sessions, which were transcribed and compiled into a book, *The Andreasson Affair* (1979), by Raymond Fowler, a member of the investigation team.

On the night in question Betty had just finished cleaning up after making supper for her seven preteen children and her parents, Waino and Eva Aho, who were visiting while Betty's husband, James, was in the hospital recovering from a car accident. The house lights began to flicker and then went out altogether. A vacuum seemed to encompass the house and all sounds stopped. From the rear kitchen window a pinkish light began to fill the house, and the Andreassons rushed to the window to see what was happening. Later Waino Aho was only able to remember seeing "Hallowe'en freaks," "small 'moon men'" who "hopped over each other like grasshoppers." The family retreated to the living room and, except for Betty, were held in a state of suspended animation, unable to move for several hours.

During the 1977 hypnotic sessions Betty recalled looking at her motionless family, then turning around to watch a group of four blue-suited aliens pass through a closed door. "I'm thinking they must be angels, because Jesus was able to walk through doors and walls and walk on water. Must be angels.... And scriptures keep coming into my mind where it says, 'Entertain the stranger, for it may be angels unaware.'" An aura of friendliness emanated from the aliens, and the tallest of them communicated by thought transference that his name was Quazgaa. Her fear diminished, Betty asked the aliens if they would like something to eat. They nodded, and she pulled some meat from the refrigerator and began to fry it on the stove. The aliens rejected the meat: "Our food is tried by fire—knowledge tried by fire.

Do you have any food like that?" Betty offered them the family Bible and "they devoured it with their eyes," flipping through the pages rapidly from front to back. In exchange, Quazgaa offered a slim blue book with luminous pages. The aliens explained that the diagrams and meaning of the blue book would be revealed to her in time, but that they could leave it with her for only a short while.

"What are you doing here?" Betty asked.

"We have come to help," the entities replied. "Will you help us? Would you follow us?"

"Are you of God?" Betty demanded. "You keep saying you have come to help the world. Why?"

"Because the world is trying to destroy itself."

"If you are of God," Betty replied, "if you are here to help and are of God, I would follow, but do not deceive me."

Betty fell into single file with the aliens and was taken outside to their ship. Looking up at the transparent bottom of the spaceship hull, she recognized the jewellike parts of the apparatus as those depicted in the blue book. Quazgaa motioned with his arm, and a hatchway opened in the side of the ship, which was now turning from transparent to opaque silver-gold. The aliens led Betty along a metallic corridor to a small platform under a blazing white light. Standing on the platform, she underwent a cleansing process as the light intensified and the platform was elevated toward the light source. Betty was then shown to a small domed room and made to change into a white examination gown. An opening at the end of a passageway revealed a hemispherical metallic room, with a high metal table in the center. Quazgaa and his assistants, who had exchanged their blue uniforms for silvery white ones, ordered Betty to lie on the table. When she protested she was "floated off her feet" and held to the table by invisible bonds. Quazgaa reassured Betty that they meant no harm and would not hurt her, but that they had to examine her and "measure her for light." A long flexible silver needle was inserted into her left nostril and into her head. When she complained of pain, Quazgaa stroked her forehead and calmed her. A second needle was inserted through her navel to probe her organs. From the ceiling a large eyelike lens descended, scanned her body, and withdrew. The examination completed, Betty was allowed to change back into her own clothes.

In subsequent hypnotic sessions Betty recounted more about her abduction. In one room of the ship she had been encapsulated in a glass module while gray fluids were flushed over her; in another room large radiating crystals bathed her in rainbow colors. At the end of her tour through the spaceship Betty was confronted with the specter of a fifteen-foot eagle that burst, phoenixlike, into flames. Within seconds the bird was reduced to ash and ember, and then, slowly, became a large gray worm. From behind her a disembodied voice called out, "Betty, you have seen and you have heard. Do you understand? I have chosen you to show the world."

"Are you my Lord Jesus? Why was I brought here?" Betty asked.

"Because I have chosen you. The time is not yet. It shall come," the voice answered.

As the aliens prepared to return Betty to her home, Quazgaa placed his hands on her shoulders and, gazing into her eyes, telepathically transmitted his thoughts to her. "He says my race won't believe me until much time has passed," Betty said. "They love the human race. And, unless man will accept, he will not be saved, he will not live.... Because of great love, they cannot let man continue in the footsteps he is going. They have technology that man could use.... It is through the spirit but man will not search out that portion."

Following the hypnotism sessions of 1977 Betty obtained a divorce from her husband. A few months later friends asked her to talk with Bob Luca, who felt that he was the victim of a "missing time" encounter with alien beings. Several months later Bob and Betty were married and settled down in Cheshire, where Bob is shop foreman in a car dealership and Betty works as a sorting clerk in a factory. Betty remains an active student of the Bible, believing that it is literal truth and that the humanoids were the messengers of God. Together she and Bob attend as many flying-saucer conventions and symposia as possible, promoting their book, The Andreasson Affair Phase 2, and counseling others who have undergone the bewildering experience of alien abduction.

Drawing by Keith Haring in the Fifty-first Street station of the Lexington IRT subway line. New York, New York.

The Flying Saucer Pie Company.
Houston, Texas.
The Flying Saucer Pie Company sells
twenty-four varieties of pie. $1.95 buys
a ten-inch pie; $5.95 buys a T-shirt
that features a flying pie beaming up
a victim with the legend, "I was abducted
at the Flying Saucer Pie Company."

More people around the world witnessed the closing ceremonies of the Twenty-third Olympic Games in Los Angeles than any other production in history—a television audience of two and a half billion.

After the lowering of the Olympic flag and the extinguishing of the flame, members of the audience were asked to switch on the flashlights they had been given as they entered the stadium. As the Coliseum filled with twinkling blue lights and the strains of *Thus Spake Zarathustra,* a glittering flying saucer with a probing searchlight appeared in the air above the stadium peristyle. A collective gasp went up from the audience. "My God, people thought *it* had arrived!" said Bob Gurr, the saucer's creator. "Ninety-three thousand people were awestruck. The idea of its being there made sense as a symbol. The reaction of the crowd certainly validated the concepts our society has of flying saucers."

Hovering over the stadium, with brilliant lights chasing around its rim, the craft signaled to earth with music and rhythmic blasts of laserlike light. A response was flashed from lights surrounding the stage in the center of the Coliseum. The ship hovered over the site for several minutes, transmitting and receiving increasingly complex and frenetic patterns of light and sound. The ship landed behind the peristyle, which glowed with bursts of red and blue light exploding between the arches, and a laser beam shot out across the stadium. The crowd oohed and aahed when a seven-foot-eight-inch white-suited alien appeared on the steps of the peristyle. "I have been watching mankind and I like what I see," said the alien to the crowd. "For almost one hundred years you have celebrated the best that humanity has to offer. You call it the Olympic Games. And for that, and for the cities that have kept the Olympic ideal alive, I SALUTE YOU!" The alien thrust his arms outward to the rolling applause of the audience and the concussion of majestic fireworks.

Video of flying saucer hovering over
the Coliseum at the Twenty-third
Olympic Games. Los Angeles,
California.

Flying saucer at the UFO & Planetary
Alignment Conference. Reno, Nevada.

A cattle barn can be a cold place. The site of the 1982 UFO & Planetary Alignment Conference was billed as the Junior Agricultural Building on the Reno Fairgrounds, but when you entered the underheated building it became apparent that this was a livestock-show arena. From the blue-draped stage, adrift in a sea of sand and trampled cow pies, the speakers gazed out across the dun-colored void to their chilled audience huddled on a slope of wooden bleachers. At one end of the arena a flying saucer constructed of aluminized Mylar shimmered under the mercury lamps. The physical set-up served as an apt metaphor for the gulf separating the miserable masses of humanity from the shining promise of visitors from outer space.

The conference was sponsored by Miguel Ribera, the prosperous owner of a Mexican restaurant in downtown Reno. For many of the middle-aged saucer fans in attendance, this "New Age Event of the Year" harked back to the halcyon days of the large UFO-contactee conventions of the 1950s and '60s. Speakers included veterans of the contactee movement such as Wayne Aho, Bob Short, and Thelma "Tuella" Terrell, coupled with relative newcomers such as Travis Walton, a prominent abductee from Arizona, and Dr. Fred Bell, a self-proclaimed former NASA engineer and holistic health expert.

The two-day event was emceed by Timothy "Mr. UFO" Green Beckley, editor of the world's only flying-saucer newspaper, *UFO Review*, and it promised to enlighten the audience about a wide range of "New Age" topics. Thelma Terrell, who channels psychic communications from the Ashtar Command, brought word of "The Secret Gathering of the Earth Based Commanders" and their discussions for global evacuation at the time of the coming world crisis. Dr. Ray Brown was scheduled to make an appearance with his "Atlantean Fire Crystal," retrieved from an underwater pyramid inside the Bermuda Triangle (he came, but refused to display the crystal). George Cogan of Star Seed Search urged spectators to undergo advanced hypnotic regression in order to reveal their lifetimes of greatest advancement and evolvement, "for those Star Seeds ready to take that next big step."

James Moseley, the lean and eccentric former editor of *Saucer News* and now editor of *Saucer Smear*, elicited the only negative reaction from the crowd during the conference. The self-styled "bad boy of UFOlogy," Moseley took the position that after thirty years of UFO sightings and testimony there still does not exist one single piece of conclusive physical evidence in support of extraterrestrial visitation. Moseley repeated his long-standing offer of $1,000 to anyone who could produce physical evidence of flying saucers. The offer was met by a disturbed rumbling from the stands, coupled with a renewed interest in the stalls and tables selling psychic-communication crystals, metaphysical tracts, and health preparations.

Bob Short of the Blue Rose Ministry in Joshua Tree, California, recounted the knowledge revealed to him since 1954 through the Space Brothers. These facts included the news that Earth, through a secret vote at the United Nations, had refused to join the Confederation of Outer Worlds, and that the desolate surface of Mars was due to a nuclear conflict there 5,000 years ago, which had forced its inhabitants into subterranean cities. Short also pointed out that the heightened anxiety over nuclear warfare expressed by New Agers is well founded and that the effects would be even worse than most people realized. "Everything exists as pairs," he explained. "Earth is the first universe. The Confederation is in the second or antimatter universe. Galaxies, planets, and solar systems and individuals too have a double in the other universe.... Balance would be disturbed if one planet is eliminated. It would create havoc in both universes! HAVOC IN *BOTH* UNIVERSES!"

In the midst of his address Short suddenly pulled his shoulders up until his chin was pressed tight against his sternum. With his eyes squeezed shut and his arms straight at his sides Short let out a deep call, "Ho-yea-ya, Ho-yea-ya! We greet you in peace, and in love."

A whispered excitement swept through the audience, "It's Korton. That's Korton speaking!"

Korton, a highly evolved being from Mars, occupies Bob Short's body and uses his vocal chords when he channels his messages to Earth. Short is unaware of what Korton is saying during these trances and cannot recall them afterward. Korton never gives advance notice of his messages, which are eagerly awaited by the regulars at the Saturday evening services of the Blue Rose Ministry. His communication at the UFO conference was deemed to be particularly prophetic.

A middle-aged woman told me that the accuracy of Korton's prophecies has stood up through the years. "I pulled up my roots in Los Angeles in two weeks' time because Korton told me, 'We have been telling you for two years to get out of the L.A. area. Now it is imperative that you relocate.' He gave me two weeks to get out of Los Angeles. In two weeks I had bought property in the mountains of northern Arizona and I've relocated there—that was a year and a half ago—on the advice of Korton."

For many of the several hundred in attendance the chance to buy aids for cosmic and physical well-being was every bit as important as listening to the speakers. Past-life readings were selling for $10, next to a display of inspirational posters of crystal civilizations and racks of "mood-sensing" pendants. Kirlian photographs, which for $10 demonstrate the depth and state of one's aura, vied for attention with $600 anti-gravity inversion benches.

Timothy Green Beckley's Global Communications conducted a brisk business selling staple-bound essays, including *New World Order: Channelled Prophecies from Space* and *The Night Mutilators*, "the horrifying story of cattle mutilations and the UFO connection." With his gold necklaces and monogrammed sunglasses, Beckley cuts a more style-conscious figure than most of the conservatively dressed participants around him. He looks very much like a rock music promoter, which he was before venturing into UFO publishing. I asked him why the Aetherians weren't participating in the conference. "UFOs can be a fun thing," Beckley responded. "I believe there's a certain entertainment aspect to it and a certain camaraderie that you get from people who are interested in the subject. But you've got to draw the line somewhere, and I draw it at George King [Aetherius] and Ruth Norman [Unarius]."

The most popular article on sale during the conference was demonstrably the Pyradome Series Headgear. These wire-framework pyramids, plated with a variety of precious and semiprecious metals, sold for $15–35 and were soon seen bobbing back and forth on the heads of many of the attendees. Invented by Dr. Fred Bell of Pyradyne Incorporated, the Pyradomes were supposed to reduce stress and air pollution, increase attention span, promote loss of appetite (for weight watchers), increase physical prowess, and engender a sense of euphoria due to the negative-ion effect. Dr. Bell maintained that people wearing Pyradomes for extended periods could effect "psychokinesis" and levitation while in higher meditative states.

"What do you call that?" asked a young woman about a complicated

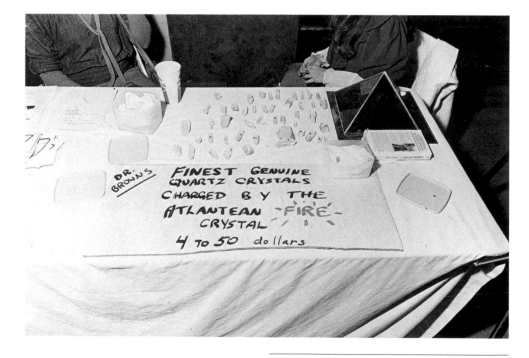

Displays at the UFO & Planetary
Alignment Conference. Reno, Nevada.

Display at the UFO & Planetary
Alignment Conference.
Reno, Nevada.

arrangement that looked like many Pyradomes wired together.

"That's the Laser model. $500 at the convention. Normally $700."

"What's it for?"

"We-use-it-for-the-accumulation-of-quantum-levels-of-energy-of-the-body," Bell recited in staccato fashion. "Turns-on-the-cellular-reproductive-capacity-of-DNA."

Walking along the row of vendors I overheard smatterings of conversations encompassing a vast range of knowledge and hope.

"It's hard to believe that some parts of *Close Encounters of the Third Kind* are so very accurate in its portrayals—I wonder what kind of knowledge Steven Spielberg has."

"DNA & RNA together . . . that's the '666' referred to in the Bible."

". . . and you notice THEY said, 'God, father of the Lights'? Now I'm a Christian and they satisfy me that they're Christian."

Two women in their early fifties approached me.

"Excuse us, but—we've been watching you—where are you from?"

"I'm from Canada."

"No, beyond that. We can tell—by your eyes—you're an old soul from somewhere else." They nodded to each other.

"I'm just here to make photographs," I said, trying to reassure them.

The elder of the two grasped one of my hands in hers. "We wanted to help you with your work." In one motion she gave me a peck on the cheek, squeezed a small, hard packet into my palm, and swept off into the crowd with her friend close behind.

In my hand was a ten-dollar bill.

The interest, efforts, and kindness of many people have made this book possible in ways too many to mention. My thanks for invaluable assistance are due Walt Andrus and MUFON, Clayton Bailey, Gray Barker, Monique Belanger and the Canada Council, Lucius Farish, George D. Fawcett, Daniel Flannery, Inc., Philip Frank, Jene Highstein, Dr. J. Allen and Mimi Hynek, David M. Jacobs, Steve Kent, Anne Leobold, Alberto Manguel, William McNeece, J. Gordon Melton and the Institute for the Study of American Religion, William L. Moore, James Moseley, John Musgrave, James E. Oberg, Jeffrey W. Perry, Renault Automobiles of Canada, John F. Schuessler, David Stupple, and Steven Yancoskie.

Special acknowledgments are due Nancy Grubb for her strength and patience, Tom Wolfe for his humor and encouragement, my wife, Kate, and my family and friends for always helping the project forward.

Acknowledgments

The UFO phenomenon attracted Lucius Farish's attention in 1957, and he has been active in the field since 1961, reviewing books on UFOs and other paranormal phenomena for magazines such as *Fate* and the *MUFON Journal*. His collection of over 5,000 volumes has taken over most of his small frame home in Plummerville. Farish also prints and distributes the *UFO News Clipping Service*, a photocopied quarterly of UFO reports garnered from the major U.S. and Canadian daily papers.

Bibliography

Adamski, George.
   Inside the Spaceships. New York: Abelard-Schuman, 1955.

_____.
   Flying Saucers Farewell. New York: Abelard-Schuman, 1961.

Angelucci, Orfeo M.
   The Secret of the Saucers. Amherst, Wisc.: Amherst Press, 1955.

Bainbridge, William S.
   The Spaceflight Revolution. New York: John Wiley & Sons, 1976.

Barker, Gray.
   They Knew Too Much about Flying Saucers: Jane Leu, W. Va.: Saucerian Press, 1956.

Bloecher, Ted.
   Report on the UFO Wave of 1947. Lawndale, Calif.: California UFO Research Institute, 1967.

Clarke, Arthur C.
   Childhood's End. New York: Ballantine, 1980.

Cohen, David.
   The Great Airship Mystery. New York: Dodd, Mead & Co., 1981.

Edwards, Frank.
   Flying Saucers—Here and Now! New York: Bantam Books, 1967.

Ellwood, Robert S.
   Religious and Spiritual Groups in America. Englewood Cliffs, N.J.: Prentice-Hall, 1973.

Festinger, Leon.
   When Prophecy Fails. Minneapolis: University of Minnesota Press, 1956.

Fowler, Raymond E.
   The Andreasson Affair. Englewood Cliffs, N.J.: Prentice-Hall, 1979.

Fry, Daniel.
   The White Sands Incident. Louisville, Ky.: Best Books, 1966.

Fuller, John.
   The Interrupted Journey. New York: Dial Press, 1966.

Godwin, John.
   Occult America. Garden City, N.Y.: Doubleday, 1972.

Hall, Richard.
   The UFO Evidence. Washington, D.C.: National Investigations Committee on Aerial Phenomena, 1964.

Hynek, J. Allen.
   The UFO Experience—A Scientific Inquiry. Chicago: Henry Regnery Co., 1972.

Jacobs, David M.
   The UFO Controversy in America. Bloomington: University of Indiana Press, 1975.

Jung, Carl G.
   Flying Saucers—A Modern Myth of Things Seen in the Sky. Princeton: Princeton University Press, 1978.

Keyhoe, Donald.
   The Flying Saucers Are Real. New York: Fawcett Publications, 1950.

_____.
   Flying Saucers—Top Secret. New York: G. P. Putnam, 1960.

King, George, and Avery, Kevin.
   The Age of Aetherius. Hollywood: The Aetherius Society, 1975.

Klass, Philip J.
   UFOs Explained. New York: Random House, 1974.

Leslie, Desmond, and Adamski, George.
   Flying Saucers Have Landed. London: Werner Laurie, 1953.

Lorenzen, Coral and Jim.
   Flying Saucers: The Startling Evidence of the Invasion from Outer Space. New York: Signet, 1966.

McNeece, William A.
   "Building a Flying Saucer: A Study in Parsonian Theory." Master's thesis, Eastern Michigan University, Ypsilanti, 1974.

Menger, Howard.
   From Outer Space to You. Jane Leu, W. Va.: Saucerian Press, 1959.

Menzel, Donald.
   Flying Saucers. Cambridge: Harvard University Press, 1953.

Newbrough, John Ballou.
   OAHSPE. Amherst, Wisc.: Amherst Press, n.d.

Reeve, Bryant and Helen.
   Flying Saucer Pilgrimage. Amherst, Wisc.: Amherst Press, 1957.

Sagan, Carl, and Page, Thornton.
   UFOs: A Scientific Debate. Ithaca, N.Y.: Cornell University Press, 1973.

Scheaffer, Robert.
   The UFO Verdict. Buffalo, N.Y.: Prometheus Books, 1981.

Scully, Frank.
   Behind the Flying Saucers. New York: Henry Holt, 1950.

Steiger, Brad.
   The Gods of Aquarius. New York: Harcourt Brace Jovanovich, 1976.

Vallee, Jacques.
   Messengers of Deception. Berkeley: And/Or Press, 1979.

_____.
   Passport to Magonia. Chicago: Henry Regnery Co., 1969.

Van Tassel, George.
   I Rode a Flying Saucer. George Van Tassel, 1952.

_____.
   When Stars Look Down. George Van Tassel, 1976.

Williamson, George, and Bailey, Alfred C.
   The Saucers Speak. Los Angeles: New Age Publishing, 1954.

Index

AT 30,000 FEET WE LEVELLED OFF AND FLASHED FOR HOME UNDER FULL ROCKET POWER.

Flying saucer at the Skycraft Surplus
Store. Orlando, Florida.